D1548998

Wifey 101

EVERYTHING I GOT **WRONG** AFTER FINDING MR. **R I G H T**

BY **JAMIE OTIS**

WITH **DIBS BAER**

© 2016 by Jamie Otis

All rights reserved. No portion of this book may be reproduced, stored in a retrieval system, photocopy, recording, scanning, or other-except for brief quotations in critical reviews or articles, without the prior written permission of the publisher.

Cover image: Johnel Felix Clemente. Editor: Shawn Fury. Cover Design: Karis Drake.

Published in New York, New York, by Jamie Otis, LLC. Jamie Otis is a registered trademark.

Print ISBN: 978-0-99736-191-9
eBook ISBN: 978-0-9973619-0-2

Printed in the United States of America

For my siblings and my husband—the most important people in my life.

FOREWORD

Fate is the optimal combination of choice and chance, said someone nobody's ever heard of on one of those inspirational Instagram memes.

My fate was decided the day I agreed to a scientifically arranged, legally binding blind marriage to Doug Hehner that was documented on television and then broadcast all over the world.

"How could you marry a complete stranger?"

That's the most common question I get from fans, friends, journalists, trolls—even my own family. It's a fair question. What kind of a person would do such a crazy thing?

A loser?

A fame whore?

A gold digger?

A lunatic?

All of the above?

In my case, the correct answer is none of the above. From the moment I was born I found myself in unusual circumstances and situations, sort of like a female, redneck version of Forrest Gump. The same can be said for the way I found myself a husband. The situation pretty much fell in my lap and I was at a place in my life where I craved love, happiness, and *family*.

I'm impulsive so I went with it. I'm also the type of person who just says it like it is. I'm brutally honest. And the truth is, I had a childhood rife with abuse, poverty, and neglect, so I craved the maternal hand-holding the panel of TV experts would provide on the show. Because of the abuse and neglect, all but one of my previous relationships were pretty much a disaster. I needed serious help if I ever wanted to have a long-term, healthy relationship. I wasn't looking for a fairy-tale family. I just wanted to be part of a family that was loving, stable, and consistent. I've never had that. I wanted it more than anything in the world.

I married Doug for better or worse and, believe it or not, I meant it with all of my heart. A lot of critics think the way I chose to be married makes a mockery of marriage. I couldn't disagree more. The divorce rate in this country still stands around 50 percent. If anything, my thought going into my scientifically arranged marriage was, "Hey, what we're doing isn't working, why not try something else?"

When I agreed to be blindly paired with a husband, I had nothing to lose. I desperately wanted it to work and I still do. I think my biggest mistake was not thinking through or realizing how ill-equipped I was to be a life partner with anyone when I signed on the dotted line. I didn't have the time or luxury of working out my immediate past or previous relationships before walking down the aisle. I truly was in over my head.

If I wanted my marriage to last, I had to learn how to be a good wife and even better in-law quickly and efficiently. If you've followed me on my journey then you know I've been less than perfect. But I hope my foibles are helpful, relatable, even inspiring. Though my marriage is unconventional (that's putting it lightly!), what I'm going through is no different than what all married couples go through— everything from silly fights over the toilet seat up or down to more serious issues like keeping deep, dark secrets from each other. You may think you've seen everything there is to know about Doug and me on TV, but there's a lot that we've kept private.

The only difference between "normal" newlyweds and me is that I had to go through all of this stuff at warp speed and make it better lickety-split while married to a complete stranger. And I'm on TV for the world to see and judge. I've written *Wifey 101* because the majority of comments I get on social media (yes, I read them all) are about comparing notes and commiserating about the art of marriage. Am I an expert? God, no. My marriage and I are both a work in progress. But I hope this helps anyone else out there who is also fumbling along trying to get it right when everything seems to be going wrong.

Here's to happily ever afters!

—Jamie Otis

CHAPTER 1

Not All Men?

Men have been an enigma to me since the day I was born. Literally. The space on my birth certificate where it says "Father" is blank.

I was in first grade when I came home from school and heard the biggest news of my short life—I was finally going to meet the man who was my daddy. I remember the day so vividly. I walked into our trailer and saw Momma at the end of the long, thin hallway, folding laundry thrown on top of the dryer. As I walked toward her, stepping over mountains of dirty clothes, she spotted me, and her eyes lit up.

"Jamie, you need to go to the doctors again," she said excitedly. "We're gonna get your blood drawn for another paternity test! I just know he has to be the one. There's nobody else it could be."

I was only six years old, but this would be my fourth paternity test. It didn't matter. I was ecstatic. Let's call him Henry. Mom said I looked just like him—he had dark brown hair and blue-green eyes, just like me. She was so certain he was my father, she sent him my most recent school photo. I was wearing a blue and white top with tiny colorful flowers on it. My bangs were brushed perfectly over my fore-head and I smiled shyly for the camera. She said I looked "real pretty" in that picture and she just knew as soon as we met I would become the "apple of his eye." I didn't really know what "apple of his eye" meant but it sounded like a good thing and I couldn't wait to meet him.

Usually men aren't exactly thrilled to hear they may have a ran-dom child—hello, Maury Povich anyone?—but Henry invited Mom and I over right away. None of the other three possible baby daddies wanted to meet me at all so I was certain this was a good sign. I dreamt about what my life would be like if Henry was my father. My mom had a different last name than I did and I was embarrassed about it. She just randomly gave me the last name of Otis, from a guy she was legally married to but separated from by the time I was born.

Would I take Henry's last name? Would I go to his place for Christmas and the other holidays? Would we eat dinner together like a real family? I smiled ear to ear at the thought of becoming a normal kid with two parents. I wanted a paved driveway and an American flag in my front yard so bad. Henry could make that happen. I'd have a daddy to come to my teacher conferences and chorus concerts. A daddy to sign the blank line meant for the "father signature" on report cards and permission slips. A daddy to show my schoolwork and art projects. I was born on Father's Day and now I would have a real one to make a gift for. I was always the only kid in class who wrote "Mom" on my Father's Day gifts.

My picture-perfect daydream turned to sheer panic when my mom and I drove over to Henry's. What if he didn't think I was as pretty as Mom thought I was in the picture? What if I wasn't nice enough? Although I was young, I was very familiar with the feeling of being inadequate. I'd already felt the devastating sting of rejection three times.

As Mom pulled in the driveway, I saw Henry's rickety white trailer sitting on a hill of weeds and overgrown grass. A couple of kids ran around in the backyard and I wondered if they were my siblings. We walked past two overflowing garbage cans and climbed up the small wooden stairs that led up to the front door. Mom knocked twice.

"Come on in!" a loud, gruff voice yelled. I grabbed Mom's hand and we walked through the door. Henry was sitting in a recliner in front of the TV, wearing a plain, blue one-pocket T-shirt covering his big ol' belly and smiling sweetly. He reminded me of Santa Claus. If Santa Claus had wicked-rotten teeth.

He wasn't exactly the Prince Charming (or Santa Claus) I'd envisioned, but I pushed that thought away.

I had so many things I'd planned on saying, but Mom did all of the talking. I stood shyly holding onto her leg, peeking out from behind her to scope out the house. The kitchen table was cluttered, and I imagined myself clearing a spot, so I could sit there and color. Mom and Henry shared a couple laughs…and that was it. After a few minutes, we were already on our way home. I never even said boo to him. As we were driving back, I was confused and upset that the visit was so short and I didn't even get to talk to my daddy. I sat in the backseat looking out the window, wondering if I'd ever get to go back. Would Henry even want to see me again? Did he hope I was his daughter, like I hoped he was my father?

A few days later Mom got a call from Henry. I sat anxiously waiting to hear what he was saying. Mom hung up and told me Henry really believed I was his child and was really excited to have me join his family! He even shared my school photo with his mother, explaining that he may have another daughter. When Henry's mother saw my photo, she told him there was no question whether or not I belonged to their family because I looked just like him when he was a kid. I was over the moon. Not only did I have a real dad, but he and my new family would welcome me with open arms and hearts.

There was only one more hurdle before my *Leave It to Beaver* fantasy came to fruition. I needed to take that paternity test.

And Momma was excited, too. She would finally stop being hounded by social services about finding my father for child support so they didn't have to give us so many food stamps. Mom was really embarrassed about that. I remember her saying, "Don't ever tell anybody about this, this doesn't make me look good."

Embarrassment went out the window when it came to a welfare check. So, a week after I met Henry, Mom took me to the medical office to get my blood drawn again for the fourth time. I wasn't scared at all. I was used to the quick little prick that felt like a bee sting. I knew it wouldn't hurt for long. As the nurse placed the tourniquet on my arm, Mom reached out to hold my hand. She rubbed my fingers and whispered in my ear, "This is it. This is the last one. We have finally found your father."

The test came back negative.

To say I was shattered would be the understatement of the century. I remember sitting on the floor of my bedroom, elbows on my knees, head in my hands, tears streaming down my face. I felt bitter, lonely, and worst of all, unwanted. As I sat there confused and crying, I begged my mom to remember anyone else who could be my father.

"Why don't I have a daddy who loves me?" I sobbed.

Mom had always been able to pull another option out of her hat. This time, when she realized it would be impossible to console me, she offered an explanation that didn't make sense to me at the time because I was so young. "I was drunk. It was late. I can remember his face in the mirror, but I just cannot remember his name."

Over the years, more details of the true story of how I was conceived would slip out. Okay, true is a strong word. Let's just say, true to my mom. Here's what I've been able to cobble together:

It was September 1985, in Mom's hometown of Freeville, New York, about 200 miles north of New York City. In the fall, "upstate" is spectacular; the air is fresh and crisp and the countryside has beautiful rolling hills with bright yellow and orange foliage. Mom was only twenty years old but she already had a one-year-old baby, my sister Johanna, father also unknown. Mom was shy and just a bit overweight and she always struggled with feeling unworthy and unaccepted, but her stepsister Sherry was a hot number, the life of the party. Mom loved hanging out with Sherry and hosting wild all-night card parties in her cozy, two-bedroom trailer. The long, grey piece of tin was in line with approximately 30 similar trailers, each sitting on cinder blocks, side by side in a loop. Trailers are notorious for having leaky ceilings, holes in the floors, and paper-thin walls. It wasn't uncommon to hear your neighbors arguing. Later in life these thin walls would prove to be life saving.

This particular night, Sherry came over to the trailer with a case of beer, Mom's favorite Seagram's wine coolers, pot, cocaine, and two men. One was Sherry's new boyfriend, the other guy—tall, dark and not very handsome, Mom recalled—she'd never met before.

As Joh slept in her playpen, propped up against the living room wall, Mom, Sherry and the guys played cards, got drunk, and got high. Mom told me she'd never tried drugs before that point but Sherry assured her it was really fun and would help her relax. Something about my mom's story already seemed suspect, especially when she said she turned down the coke because Joh was in the room.

The group partied until the sun came up, and the booze and drugs ran out. Tired and out of it, Mom changed into her nighty and went to the bathroom to get ready to go to sleep. She thought everyone left. "I began to brush my teeth," she said. "When I looked up in the mirror, I saw him standing there behind me. That's all I remember. I must have blacked out."

It took me becoming an adult before I fully understood the gravity of what my mom might have been trying to tell me: I was the product of a rape. When I flat out asked her, she said quietly, "I don't know." One clue leads me to believe it was: Did Mom ever ask Sherry how to get in contact with this guy? Surely, Sherry would remember his name. But Mom said she never asked. How did Mom have fun with this guy all night, remember what he looked like, and still not know his name? It didn't make any sense to me then and definitely doesn't now.

Hearing a shortened version of this story when I was a small kid just brought another bout of painful tears. The feeling of rejection and being unloved overtook me. I don't know why, since this man didn't necessarily even know I was alive, but that didn't stop me from experiencing soul-crushing heartache. I'd bragged to Johanna, "Nyah nyah nyah nyah nyah, I have a dad"—my older sister was *always* bullying me—and it was like finally, I have one up on her. I couldn't even think about facing her now.

I cried so hard I shook uncontrollably and got the hiccups. Mom pulled me onto her lap and started rocking me. She wiped my tears away and began combing her fingers through my hair. I was so thankful to have my mommy. I knew she loved me. I felt protected by her.

"Will you always be there for me?" I asked her. "Will you always be my mommy?"

"Baby girl," she answered, "after you were born I took one look at you and knew I was going to love you and keep you forever."

That was an odd thing to say. Why wouldn't my mom "keep" me? More on this later…

"You have a step-daddy," she then reminded me. "He loves you."

Right, my stepfather Hank—not his real name. I nodded my head in agreement, because I didn't want my mom to love me less if I disagreed. The truth was, I was terrified of Hank and pretty much every other male in the first decade of my life. Men went from being mysterious to monsters. Here's why: Five years after I was born, my mom married Hank, a son of a cop and, frankly, a son of a bitch. He drank too much and smoked weed and was always in trouble with the law. But my mom couldn't resist his dark curls and hazel eyes and she really liked the fact that he "accepted" Joh, my younger sister AmyLynn (father also unknown until she turned sixteen), and me as his own. Plus, Mom got pregnant with twins Dale and Leah, so they tied the knot in front of a justice of the peace with a couple family members present and moved into a new trailer in Beacon View.

We did not have a good life with Hank as our "daddy."

As I sit here and write this I am trying to think of any fond memories I have of Hank. Honestly, I can only think of one. He was watching the news one night and I crawled up onto his lap and put my head on his chest. I could hear his breathing and his heart beating, so I tried matching my breaths with his but he was breathing so slowly I had to take extra breaths. That was the only time I cuddled with Hank and felt safe. Beyond that, I never felt comfortable or settled in his presence. I don't remember him showing any interest in us, ever playing with us, or teaching us anything. But Mom swears he was a good father, at least a better father than a husband.

My most vivid memory of Hank was him sitting at the kitchen table smoking cigarettes and bossing us kids around like a drill sergeant. He made us do the same chores over and over again. Vacuuming, picking up toys, laundry, sweeping, mopping. One time he made me rewash the dishes for hours because I didn't wash them the right way the first time.

The worst memory of Hank was him punching and beating the snot out of my mom and nearly killing her.

Hank was a garbage man at one point but he never had a steady job. Whenever he wasn't working, which was a lot, he drank all day long—he always had a can of Budweiser in his hand. And whenever he drank, that's when all hell broke loose.

For example, one summer night, I woke up to the shrill screeches of Mom and Hank fighting. Joh and I snuck down the hallway and when we got to the bathroom, we saw Hank standing on top of my mom on the bathroom floor, his giant hands pushing her neck against the edge of the bathroom tub. Her face was purple. She was lying there limp, as if she'd given up. She wasn't trying to wiggle herself loose from him or kick or fight back. Instantly I knew what was happening. He was trying to choke her to death. My heart pounding, I ran away terrified. But Joh went right in there and punched her tiny fists into his big back, yelling as loud as she could into his ear, "Leave my mommy alone!" Hank suddenly let go of Mom's neck and turned toward Joh, who ran for her life. As he chased after her through the trailer, Mom snapped out of her trance and screamed for us to hide in her room. Everything after that is a blur to me. Eventually the police showed up and took Hank to jail.

Usually when they were fighting, my mom always went to us for protection because he never beat us. I did get painful spankings when he found out I was a bed-wetter. He despised me wetting the bed. Every time I wet the bed he would grab me, throw me over his knee and begin smacking his hand or a belt or a spatula or a wooden spoon hard on my bottom. "Come here!" he'd snarl. "You will not keep wetting the bed!"

I tried my hardest not to wet the bed. I'd lay there, eyes closed tight, repeating a mantra to myself: "Don't wet the bed. Don't wet the bed. Wake up to pee! Wake up to pee!" It was no use though. I'd still wake up in the middle of the night or the next day with a sodden mattress and sheets. I would silently cry and try to figure out a way to hide it from Hank. I eventually came up with what I thought was a genius plan. When I wet the bed I would just make it as if nothing happened. Then I'd stuff my pajamas at the very bottom of the dirty laundry basket so he wouldn't see them, feel them, or smell them. It didn't take Hank long to catch on. One morning, I was watching cartoons in the living room when I heard him scream, "Jamie!" I knew instantly I was in big trouble. I walked down the hallways and saw him holding up my dirty, urine-soaked PJs.

"What's this?" he sneered with the coldest, meanest eyes.

"I don't know." Wrong answer. Tears streamed down my face.

"You tried to hide this, huh? You're going to learn!"

I slowly backed away, saying, "I'm sorry. I didn't mean to!" But he had zero sympathy. He took my arm and yanked me down the hallway, carrying my pajamas in his other hand. He took me right out through the living room in front of my sisters and brother, took off his belt, lay me over his knees, and beat my bottom until it was covered in red welts. With each hit I would yell for mercy, but he just kept lashing away.

"This is what you get for trying to hide," he said. "You're going to learn to stop acting like a two-year-old!"

So, yes, Hank spanked me, and one time he threw my sister out into the snow by her arm and dislocated her shoulder. But my mom got it way worse. This was normal life for my family: Hank getting drunk, beating my mom, the police hauling him off to the can. Mom rarely pressed charges and, after he'd calmed down behind bars, we'd go visit Hank in jail during visiting hours—get all dressed up in our best clothes and bring snacks and books to the man who almost just murdered our mother.

"I'm so sorry," he'd cry, crocodile tears struggling to squeeze out of his eyeballs. "I didn't mean it. You guys are my everything. You are my whole world."

Hank never stayed in jail too long and the time that he was away was like the equivalent of a vacation in Jamaica. But we knew he'd come around again, it was like the never-ending, impending doom of a hurricane. So we kids cherished the happier, calm times we had alone with Mom. Joh and I would always follow her into the bathroom, hang out in there and chitchat, even when she was pooping. Eventually, Mom would drop the bomb (not that bomb, ew).

"You know Daddy is getting out of jail soon," she'd say. "Do you want him to come back and live with us again?"

"No!" we'd beg. "Please, Mom, don't let him live with us!"

Surprise, she always ended up letting him live with us. On some level, I understand why. She was afraid that if Hank left she'd be alone with five children to feed. Mom didn't seem to have much support from family. I remember she told me that she felt like the "black sheep" of the family because she had gotten pregnant with us kids out of wedlock. That was highly frowned upon. With little support from family I guess it's understandable why she'd go to the one man who "loved" her so much regardless of the mistakes she'd made.

I remember after Hank would get sprung, he'd come home with a big smile, teeth yellowed from chew and cigarettes. I despised that smile. I knew it wouldn't be long before it'd turn into a vicious evil frown and he'd go on an angry rampage. He also cheated on my mom. There were so many nights when Hank would go out drinking and Mom would sit home furious.

"I just know he's cheating on me with another girl," she'd fret. "I'm no dummy!"

She became obsessed with the idea of "catching him in the act." We became her PI assistants. Didn't matter if it was 2 a.m. or in the middle of a blinding snowstorm, we were gonna go hunt down Daddy. We'd throw our coats on over our pajamas and climb into our station wagon, cold, confused, and exhausted. One time, Mom drove to every bar in the area until she saw his rusty truck parked at a local dive that looked like a barn. As she skidded into the parking lot, the light of the neon signs burned our sleepy eyes. Mom put the wagon in park and left it running so the heat could stay on for us kids while she went inside to catch our daddy. She swung the bar door open, loud music wafted out into the chilly night air, and she stormed in to confront him. I was petrified for her. Hank would no doubt be drunk and God help her if he was in a dark mood. I sat in the backseat shaking from the cold and my nerves, staring at the bar door, praying she would come out alive. Eventually she did come out. With Hank screaming and hollering right behind her. Mom would climb in the car with her face wet from crying.

Of course, the jerks who cheat always accuse their partners of cheating and Hank was no exception to that rule. One night, during a brief period when my mom had kicked him out, he came around wasted to terrorize us all.

"Whore!" he hollered in our front yard for the whole trailer park to hear. Then he pounded on the door, demanding my mother let him in to see "my kids." What a joke.

"You have no right to see the kids until you're sober!" she shouted. "Come back when you're not drunk or I'll call the police!"

This only made him more irate.

"Cop-caller!" he roared. He was always calling her a "cop-caller," like it was an insult.

Hank threw his whole body into the flimsy door and it busted open.

"I'm taking my kids!"

Joh and I hid in the hallway watching Mom and Hank scream at the top of their lungs at one another. He accused her of sleeping around on him. Hank tried stomping down the hall to the twins' bedroom but my mom threw herself in front of him. She always tried protecting us from his violence. He tried to shove her away but she wouldn't budge. That's when he grabbed his shotgun.

"I'm going to fucking kill you!" He stormed into the living room and put the barrel on the wall. On the other side was the twins' room. "I am going to fucking kill everyone!"

Mom ran over to Hank and pushed the gun away from the wall. He held the gun up to her head and cocked the shotgun. All of us—Mom, Joh, AmyLynn, even the baby twins—wailed hysterically. "I'll fucking kill you!" he spit. "You know I will!"

Before Hank could shoot all of us dead, our neighbors quietly broke into the trailer and carried the babies out the back door. Then they bravely snuck back in to escort the rest of us out. Someone called 911, I have no idea who. The police arrived and confiscated Hank's weapons, and he was hauled off to jail yet again. I watched through the neighbors' window blinds as the officers cuffed him and threw him in the cop car—the blue and red lights flashing through the window. When he turned his head toward the trailers, I was scared to death he'd see me. I ducked down low to hide from him. The siren and lights faded away and I finally felt safe. Thank God it was over. This time.

Sometimes Mom would pretend that she was done with Hank and go on dates with other guys. Terrible idea for everyone involved. Like poor, unsuspecting Larry. Actually, Larry wasn't such a rube. He had two teardrop tattoos under his eye and cherries on his arm with the words, "I got my cherries, where are yours?" I remember asking him what it meant and he asked if I had my cherries. Anyway, Larry took all of us to the county fair one night while Hank was in jail. After he bought us all the sweet cotton candy and rides we could dream of, Mom let him in on her little secret.

"I heard Hank got outta jail early," she told a stunned Larry. "I'm scared if he did he's gonna come looking for us." Then she turned to us kids. "Let me know if you see Daddy because he's not going to be happy we're here with Larry."

We were on the top of the Ferris wheel when, sure enough, we spotted Hank, fresh out of jail. Mom panicked. "As soon as the Ferris wheel stops, get out and run to the car!" she whispered. "Your daddy is here and he is real mad." I was so sad we had to leave the fair but I also knew things were about to get really ugly if we didn't hightail it out of there. As soon as the Ferris wheel stopped, we walked as fast as we could to our car without Hank spotting us. But, just like in a horror movie, as we were pulling out of the field, a big car came speeding up behind us. It was Hank. Clearly he was drunk. He was riding the rear of our car, bumping into it and honking his horn like a lunatic. He was trying to get my mom to pull over. Mom knew if she pulled over, he would try to fight Larry or worse. She sped up but Hank drove on the wrong side of the road, got right next to us, and tried to ram us off the road. Then Mom and Hank both slammed on the brakes at the same time. Hank ran up to our car, climbed up on the hood, and pulled out a knife.

"Be a man!" he shouted at Larry, pounding the windshield. "Face me like a man!" Larry's cherries shriveled up and he sat there paralyzed with fear.

As soon as Hank got off the hood, Mom quickly sped off and drove right to the police station. She knew that was the only place he wouldn't follow us. We all just sat there crying, catching our breath. Larry was still speechless. I wasn't sure if I was happy he didn't get out and fight, or if I felt like he was a complete loser for not protecting us. Either way, apparently he had no idea what he was getting into when he began dating my mom. That was the end of Larry. And other guys, as long as Hank was around.

Instead of dating new guys, one time while Hank was in the clink, Mom got a teacup poodle named Tiffany for companionship. Well, when Hank came back, he was not pleased about that either. He claimed my mom loved the puppy more than him and, during a drunken rage, right in front of us, threw it across the room into a corner of our TV and the glass mirror behind it. She looked like she broke her neck and was bleeding out of her mouth and nose. The dog lay limp, whimpering in pain. She wasn't quite dead yet so Hank and his friend tried crushing up some pain pills to feed her. My sister Joh said the SPCA came to mercy kill the dog, but Mom said they were too late. The dog had already died.

Mom finally wised up and, thankfully, mercy killed the marriage. Murdering her dog apparently crossed the line and was the final straw. She packed up the station wagon and just left the trailer to Hank, deserved or not.

If this was a Hollywood movie ending, our family would be rewarded for leaving our mother's abuser and everything would be swell. We might even end up with a new nice dad and a big house with a kitchen like Anne Hathaway had in *The Intern*. But if I'm being completely truthful, I can't say that life got easier after Mom left Hank. In fact, it got worse. At this point, the most influential man in my life was the guy who beat the crap out of my mom. The next man to have a major impact on me was my molester. Strike two.

Over the next decade, we moved about 11 times, always because we'd been evicted, and I went to six different schools. Most trailer park people are poor folks struggling to pay their bills, living paycheck to paycheck, just trying to survive. The majority of these families need government checks for heat, food, and rent. Mom wasn't an exception. She tried to do well as a good single parent but there just weren't enough hours in a day for her to give enough attention to each child or the housework.

Neighbors and teachers called Child Protective Services at least three times. Joh and I were in a school program called "Banana Splits" for children who had divorced parents. I think my Banana Splits counselor was on to us because my mom told me not to share anything about our lives with her. She didn't trust her. They all figured it out anyway. The first time CPS was called, someone claimed we didn't have food. But when the social worker showed up at our trailer, Mom flung open the freezer and all the cupboards to show her that we had more than just powdered milk. "See, we have food!" she said defensively. Luckily, Mom had just gotten her food stamps and stocked up.

Mom hated CPS but also used them to discipline us. I remember one time when Joh and I were acting up, we told her we were running away. "Go ahead!" Mom screamed. "Go pack your bags!"

"Come on, Jamie, let's go get our stuff!" Joh said. We ran into our bedroom and packed our toys in big, black trash bags. When we came back out to the living room, Mom was on the phone pretending to be talking to CPS. "Don't worry, they're coming to get you!" she taunted.

Joh wasn't scared, but I broke down and wailed, "Don't let them take me, Momma!"

As life got more out of control, our trailers got increasingly more cluttered and run down. There were always dirty dishes in the sink, mountains of laundry, and mice. We were very proud we never got roaches from the neighbors. Mom said those little buggers traveled fast so we always made sure to shake our clothes off after hanging out at our friends' trailers. We may have had a cluttered, messy house with occasional mice, but we never had a bad case of roaches. We killed them off the first time we saw them crawling up the wall.

Mom had a lot of jobs but rarely kept one for long. In the beginning we never went hungry, though our diets consisted of peanut butter, Ramen noodles, and fast food. We used food stamps (which always embarrassed my mom) and got free meals at school (I was always embarrassed about that). All staples came from the local food pantry. For holiday dinners, we'd go to churches handing out free turkeys and stuffing. A lot of times we woke up and it was freezing in the house because our electricity had been turned off.

It never bothered me. I didn't know any different. When I was a kid, my mom was like a superhero to me. She always protected us from Hank. She always told us how much she loved us. I never thought about the fact that we lived in so many different places or that we were considered dirt-poor trailer trash. I thought my Momma was the most amazing woman. She was so beautiful to me. She had long blond feathered hair and was a bit heavier than the average woman, which made her extra cozy for hugs and snuggling on the couch. She had blue-green eyes, which she insisted changed depending on her mood. I'd always plop myself down on our teeny-tiny bathroom floor and watch as she applied her makeup. I watched as she smiled to sweep her rosy powdered blush on her cheekbones. She'd lean over the sink to get closer to the mirror so she could smother each lash plump with mascara. She took her sweet time making sure she looked pretty, even if she was just going to the grocery store. Mom insisted she wanted to look presentable.

That was her biggest downfall. Men were always more important to her than anything, including her children. At least when Hank was around, Mom was home and attempting to take care of all of us. But when she became single again, she changed.

The first thing I noticed was a major change in her wardrobe. She started wearing shorts with her butt cheeks hanging out. And she'd stuff her boobs—which Momma said sagged down to her belly button because she had to breast-feed five babies—into those low-cut shirts. I would always yell at her, "Put some clothes on!" I was so embarrassed of it. I've always found cleavage and booty shorts disgusting, not sexy.

She also started partying a lot again, throwing her card games at our trailer, even on weeknights, with her boobs and butt hanging out, cackling with her friends. At some point, she started doing drugs, pot and cocaine at first, but later it progressed to crack. There wasn't a door on my bedroom and it was so loud and bright and all the lights would be on and she didn't care. I'd try to cover my eyes and ears and nose and get to sleep for school, but would end up frustrated, yelling, "Please keep it down!"

"Leave us alone!" my mom would yell back. "Stop acting like you're my mother!"

The worst side effect of Mom's new life was that new men—strangers really—were coming and going constantly. She'd have noisy sex when I was hanging out with a friend in the living room and I'd have to turn up music to drown it out. If I complained, she'd tell me to "mind my own business," or even more traumatizing, she'd go to the guy's house and leave us all in the car while she went inside to have sex.

"You are not to get out of this car under any circumstances," she scolded us. "Do not embarrass me." Sometimes she'd bring Joh inside with her because she knew she'd honk the horn obnoxiously or just barge in anyway. I always wanted to please her so I'd say, "Okay, Mommy! Guys quiet down!" even though we'd have to sit in the car bored out of our skulls for what seemed like hours. I liked being the good girl.

I don't know if it was the drugs or what, but it seemed like my mother stopped caring about my siblings and me. She stopped going to parent-teacher conferences and started pawning us off on other people to take care of us. When I was in Girl Scouts, my mom could never come because she couldn't find a babysitter, and she was always late to pick me up. A couple times she completely flaked and the Girl Scout leader had to drive me home. She walked me up to the door and said, "Here's Jamie," and my mom was like, "Oh, I forgot tonight was Brownies." I could tell my Girl Scout leader was like, "How is it six at night and you don't notice your kid is missing?" When Joh's rebellion got out of control, Mom said she couldn't handle her and she made her go live with a boyfriend she dated for like a month. I felt bad Joh had to go live with this strange ex-boyfriend alone so I told her I'd go too. Apparently all Mom had to do was offer to let him claim us on his taxes and he'd take us in. I guess he felt bad for us.

You can only imagine the result of all of these older, un-vetted men going in and out of our lives and our trailers. The irony is that my mom used to tell us girls, "Don't trust men, they only want one thing." At least three of us kids were molested—that I know of for sure. The story of my molestation, which started around the age of seven and didn't end until I was ten, is so dark and shameful to me, this is the first time I'm even acknowledging it anywhere other than in my mind and my memories.

One of my mom's crushes during the time right after Hank left was a teenage boy, we'll call him Frank, about 18, who lived in our trailer park. Remember, my mom was only about 28 at the time. All the kids would play kickball in the common circle and I didn't know what flirting was, but I could tell that my mom thought highly of him. So then *I* thought highly of him. I remember I was so flat chested and I would try to push my nonexistent boobs together to get him to notice me.

He did notice me and several other young girls in our trailer park. I found out later not only did he molest me, he molested one of my sisters and my friend. It usually happened at his house when no one was there but he also cornered me in a drugstore once, too. He would make me kiss him and give him hand jobs and oral sex. He would tell me what he liked and I would do it. He ejaculated in my mouth and I didn't know what was spewing out. My mouth was always just wet. It was disgusting, just disgusting. I didn't even know what an orgasm was. I just knew I felt like I had to make him happy and proud of me. Isn't that twisted and weird? And the thing that's even more messed up is that for awhile I'd be upset if I didn't feel like

I made him happy or if he didn't pay attention to me later when I'd see him around the trailer park. I was like, "What did I do wrong?"

My mom didn't use her best judgment and actually hired Frank to babysit us. My sister said she told her what he was doing to the girls in the trailer park but my mom didn't believe her. When he came over, we'd all watch cartoons together and I'd try to sneak away so he couldn't get to me. I'd go sleep in my mom's bed, thinking he wouldn't dare touch me or do anything with me there. No such luck. He ignored my claims of being sleepy and insisted on kissing me goodnight and tucking me in, which led to groping and more abuse.

I always felt like what happened was my fault because I put myself in situations where he could do these things to me. Am I the one who actually wants this or is he manipulating me to think that I want this? Because that's kind of what happened. I know logically what I'm saying doesn't make sense. Of course at that age, this wasn't my fault. But ever since then it just really screwed with my head because I technically wasn't forced. I could have avoided going to his house or being anywhere near him.

The abuse went on for years and didn't stop until we moved out of Beacon View, the first and only time we moved to a house with stairs. I felt gross and disgusted and ashamed. The only thing that made me feel good about it was if he would praise me afterwards. After a while, nothing about it made me feel good. I knew it felt wrong. This same sort of thing happened again later on, but with a different boy. This time I was older and wiser. I remember lying down in my mom's bedroom with her and another trailer park boy. He had been flirting with me, but it seemed innocent. We were watching a movie together when he began rubbing my back. His rubs began getting lower and lower on my back. I remember lying there secretly hoping it would stop. I felt paralyzed like I couldn't move or speak. I sat there quiet while inside I was screaming "STOP IT!" I don't know why I couldn't just say it out loud. Mom got up to go to the bathroom and I quickly jumped up to follow her into the room. As she was peeing I whispered to her that he began rubbing my back and I didn't feel comfortable. She said, "Let me sit between you two so it doesn't happen again." I was hoping she would just kick him out, but that worked too.

Many have wondered why I have trust issues. Most people just feel bad for my husband, Doug. He would get so frustrated when I didn't immediately trust him in our relationship. It's not an excuse but this is what I grew up with. I pride myself on talking openly and honestly—regardless of how bad my flaws make me look—but this is way too heavy to just bring up in a nonchalant conversation. It's not easy to talk about.

So why am I telling this story now? As I type this, Doug knows something crappy happened to me but he doesn't know the details. It's a bad memory, I don't want to see it in my head. I don't want to go there at all. But I will tell him before this book is published because secrets in a relationship—or anywhere in life—are unhealthy. And I've kept too many from him (See CHAPTER 6). I've learned that keeping dark skeletons in your closet only causes shame and hurt. The moment you open up and share them is the moment you realize that you're not alone, that there are others who are hiding ugly secrets, too. When you finally let them go, you can find others who understand. Together you can lean on each other for support.

My goal in sharing my story is that it inspires you. And I'm telling you because it helps explain why I'd choose to seek a husband the way I did. My love life—until I got married—was a disaster, a direct result of the abuse I witnessed and experienced from Hank and Frank. After my molestation happened, I went the complete opposite direction with men. I never felt comfortable or safe around them. I didn't want a boyfriend. I only liked guys that were not interested in me—not because I liked the chase but because I felt safer with them. You would not believe how awkward I am sexually (still to this day).

It took me 27 years—and going on an extreme reality show experiment that arranges marriages—to figure out that my past didn't have to control and/or ruin my future.

I'm living proof that you can find happiness, if you've been in a similar situation. But it takes a lot of hope and even more work.

As scared as I was of real intimacy, I never gave up on finding true love.

CHAPTER 2

Love In A Hopeless Place

A bandoned, neglected, and abused. Sounds like a band name—hey, bro, A.N.A. put on a killer show at Irving Plaza last night! I'm making a joke because sometimes that's easier than dealing with the pain. But it's not a band, it's a summary of the first decade of my life.

Between my mother and the sorry excuses for the male species roaming around like wild animals in my trailer park, I had zero positive role models when it came to loving relationships. Which left it up to me to figure it out on my own. Good luck with that, scared little girl!

JAMIE OTIS | Wifey 101

It didn't help that the first boy I ever liked rejected me. His name was Brian and he was my kindergarten class's cow-licked cutie. Wow, that was some serious alliteration. Anyway, every girl liked him and we all raced each other to the school bus so we could snag the seat next to him. Well, flash-forward to the school dance, he asked this girl Kirsten if she was down with O.P.P. instead of me and I was crushed.

After Brian, I never really had crushes. The molestation nightmare happened not long after and pretty much destroyed that innocent part of me for a long time. I wanted nothing to do with any guy. In fact, in ninth grade I pretended to like Jason, the one guy I thought had zero interest in me, so I didn't seem weird to my boy-crazy friends. I was always more concerned with the girls liking me than the guys. But the girls didn't like me either, probably because they knew I was trailer trash. The first day of school, all the girls would show off their expensive new clothes and sneakers and I would try to hide my feet because I had those generic white canvas shoes from Walmart, which just screamed loser, and I was wearing hand-me-downs from my cousin LouAnn. I loved getting the bags filled with my cooler, older cousin's clothes. I thought they were awesome, but apparently I was the only one.

I wanted to be included so I claimed Jason as my crush. He was totally out of my league—he had spiky hair that he dyed different colors but he wasn't wild. He was a nice, respectful churchgoer, who was more into doing tricks on his bike than doing girls. He barely knew

I existed so I felt so safe around him. I actually started to like him for real. When he walked me home one day, I was excited but terrified he'd try to kiss me. I was too ashamed to do anything remotely sexual. I felt gross and like a big phony acting all shy and demure waiting for a simple peck on the lips. If he knew the disgusting things I'd done, he wouldn't want anything to do with me. Nobody would. Or should. A horrible thing to say about myself, but that's how I felt. I still kind of do now.

Jason didn't live in our trailer park and that's another reason why I wisely chose him as my crush. He wouldn't be around a lot and he wouldn't want to come over. That was my pattern from grade school throughout high school—find the boys who weren't interested in me and didn't live near me because I didn't want them to come over. I was too worried about the impromptu wild parties there and ashamed of my filthy house. Or should I say houses. We were evicted from every trailer park in the area—Congers, Hanshaw Village, Beacon View—and moved more than 11 times during this part of my life. I changed schools practically every year in middle and high school.

We lived in so many different places and my mom had so many different boyfriends, many with old school country singer names like Jimbo, Sterly, or Marty...but none of them stuck around long. Sterly was a truck driver and sometimes after a long road trip, we'd hear his big rig rolling up to the trailer. "He's here!" Mom would shout. "Hurry, clean the house!" We needed a lot longer than the five frantic minutes it took him to park that big boy to wash the crusted dishes stacked haphazardly in the sink, or find a new location for the piles of trash and dirty clothes covering every inch of the trailer. Sterly ended up kicking Mom to the curb, probably because she was a lazy piece of poo and the house was a pigsty. It's too bad because he was a decent guy who worked hard. Mom, on the other hand, couldn't keep a job to save her life, so we got used to having the electricity and heat shut off, often in the dead of winter. In sixth grade, after Sterly dumped Mom but kept the trailer, we moved into an apartment out of our school district, not long before the end of the school year. Rather than risk me having to repeat the grade, my mom let me live at a horse ranch up the road owned by a friend's father.

Dean was a single dad taking care of his daughter and he was the best man I'd ever met in my life. I was always skittish around men, and at first I was scared he would do something to me, but he never did. He showed me what a normal family was like. He'd get home from work, and while he made dinner, he made us do our homework. Sometimes he even took us to Friendly's for ice cream afterwards. I loved being told to do my homework and chores because nobody ever had. It's funny because I always craved rules and boundaries. I made sure I did my homework and got good grades. I used to pretend I had a curfew even though I could've stayed out until the sun came up and the roosters crowed. If I was out and my friend had a rule that she couldn't drive past 9 p.m., I said I had the same rule and had to go home, too. The truth was, I could've driven to Vegas or joined the circus and nobody would have cared or even noticed I was gone. Actually this happened. Not joining the circus but fast-forward to when I was a teenager, a group of "cool guys" from the neighboring high school asked me if I wanted to drive to Myrtle Beach in South Carolina for spring break that night. They were sneaking away, without telling their parents. I wanted to go, too. So, I went home, packed my bags, tapped my mom on the shoulder to wake her up, and told her I was headed to Myrtle Beach for a week with some guy friends. She said, "Okay, honey, have fun," rolled over and went back to sleep. I lied to the guys and told them I "snuck out" just to try and fit in.

When summer came, I ended up leaving Dean's wonderful house, because I missed my mom. I know, I know, it may sound nuts but she was my mom no matter what and I still really loved and respected her. I knew she was legitimately trying to be the best mom she could be. But now, looking back, I don't even think she realized how her actions were so hurtful and life-changing. Like, nobody ever taught me about the birds and the bees. I learned about sex being molested and seeing my mom and her boyfriends doing it on the living room couch. One time I had a friend over and we overheard my mom moaning and groaning in the next room. Mortified and my face beat red, I banged my elbow on the wall to get her to quiet down.

"Mom! We can hear you!"

"Mind your own business!" she yelled back. "Turn the music up!"

These incidents traumatized me and made me not interested in sex even slightly, which got harder to avoid the older I got. Boys liked me in high school but I kept them at a distance, especially if they were loud and rowdy. I didn't feel safe with those kinds of guys. Like, this one popular kid wanted to ask me to a dance. "She looks like Britney Spears," he told my friend on the cheerleading squad (I did every activity I could to be normal). "She's so beautiful, I would love to go with her."

"That's so lame," I told my friend when she relayed his compliment, even though inside I was twirling around in glee that someone thought I was pretty. I was just trying to protect myself. I knew that he'd dated another girl named Amanda and they had sex. Meanwhile I thought he was so handsome and he treated Amanda so well. He always got her nice little gifts and stuff like that. I wanted that so badly but I was too scared. So I just pretended I didn't like him at all. Some guys actually thought I was too good for them and even called me snobby or preppy, usually in a flirtatious way. Even my mom and sister Joh were straight up mean to me about the fact that I was always brushing my hair, took long showers and spent extra time making myself look presentable. I never wanted to come across as "too good" to anyone, but I knew I didn't want the life I'd grown up with. A lot of these guys smoked cigarettes and wore grungy clothes and smoked pot. Inside, I was like, "That's not for me." I admit I tried to hide the ugly truth of my poverty. I remember once I made my mom give a friend $50 as a graduation present because anything else seemed like nothing compared to the $200 checks most people handed out. Meanwhile, we had duct tape holding our broken windows in place and had this water contraption outside because social services determined our landlord had been giving us dirty water to drink.

Finally, by tenth grade, I built up my courage and shared my first real kiss with a harmless boy named Cory. Not long after, I had my first "real" boyfriend Kraig. We dated for nine months but I never once invited him over to my house. We only kissed and held hands—it never went anywhere else. It could have gone further two times but I stopped it. We were in his basement, naked in the pitch black, but I still needed to keep my eyes closed so tight. I really liked Kraig and trusted him, but I kept tensing up and he kept backing off.

"Are you sure?" he asked me gently several times.

"I'm so sorry, I can't do it."

He put his pants back on, went upstairs and let me get dressed. Kraig was a senior but he graduated a virgin because of me. Okay, he did lie and ended up telling his friends we slept together, but I don't blame him. He was so respectful to me in the moment and I'm grateful for that.

I fell in love for the first time my senior year of high school with a boy we'll call Ted, who played basketball at a local community college. Around the same time, my mom was on a downward spiral, a full-blown addict who was smoking crack and disappearing for weeks at a time. I was extremely depressed that whole year. Most of my classmates were excited about going away to college and I had no idea what to do. On the outside, nobody would have had any idea. I did my best to try to fit in and look normal. By high school, I had a lot of friends and was the head cheerleader (I don't know how I got that. I guess I was reliable and hard working). The truth was, I was desperately trying to survive and make sure my siblings were okay. I clung on to Ted, the only person I felt loved me, for dear life. At first he treated me like a queen, buying me chocolates and a teddy bear for Valentine's Day. He wanted to take me to a movie and when I told him I felt bad doing something fun without my siblings, he said they could go, too. It's not surprising that I lost my virginity to him the summer after I graduated high school—I'd do anything to keep him.

We dated for three years and I really was blindly in love with Ted. He came from a decent, churchgoing family so his parents were suspicious of me, because they were super religious. At one point, I had no heat, water or electricity, so Ted asked his parents if I could shower at their place. It got so bad that I was being picked on about my hygiene. Girls at school would say, "Someone smells like pee," and it was obviously me they were talking about. During this time, I'd try to plan out whose house I could shower at. I'd go to my friend's, then wait a couple days and use another friend's shower, then wait a few days and try to use Ted's. I didn't want these families to feel like I was just using them for their showers or overusing their showers. My one friend's mom would ask me to make it quick because they had a well that would dry up if too much water was used. It made me feel awful that I was using their water. But, it also made me feel so grateful that they'd let me shower there.

Ted's parents didn't know how bad it was. They were so conservative, they usually said I couldn't shower there because I'd be naked in their home. Ted and I didn't even dare kiss in front of them. Little did they know that we'd sneak sex sessions in Ted's bedroom. We were so quiet; we could hear his dad snoring through the wall. It was so scandalous and I did think it was kind of hot because it was so bad and I was such a goody-goody.

I'm making it sound like we were love machines but we *so* were not. I never really enjoyed sex with Ted and never had an orgasm. I was still grossed out and traumatized by it all and often couldn't follow through. One time we were getting hot and heavy and I pulled out the "I can't" card. He was furious. He put his hand right next to my head, stared in my eyes and seethed, "You bitch." That was my first sign that maybe Ted wasn't such a great guy.

He was inexperienced and had no idea what he was doing and neither did I. I didn't want to know. What I did know was that I needed to be on birth control because the way my family popped out babies was nuts. I scheduled an appointment with my pediatrician who I called Dr. Vitale, even though I think she was technically a nurse practitioner. I peed in the cup and sat on the chair with the loud, crinkly wax paper, reading flyers on the walls while I waited for her to come in. Dr. Vitale came bouncing in with her big smile and gentle approach. I told her I began having sex and wanted to know what type of birth control pill she'd recommend. As we were discussing options there was a knock on the door. She ignored the knock and we continued to discuss the different options. Someone knocked again, only louder this time. When Dr. Vitale opened the door there was a nurse on the other side. She needed to speak with her privately.

When Dr. Vitale walked back in she didn't have that same big grin on her face.

"Jamie, you're pregnant."

She said it just as plainly and bluntly as that. I looked at her like she'd just spoken Chinese. I couldn't even comprehend what she was saying. How could I be? We only had sex a few times, and I always insisted on using a condom, except for one time when we used the "pull-out method." I was dumbfounded. I was only eighteen.

"You have options," Dr. Vitale continued.

I couldn't even speak. I stared down at my feet.

"It isn't uncommon for a girl your age to choose abortion since it's still very early."

Abortion? No way! I knew that was a sin. It was absolutely unacceptable in church and even with my friends and my family.

"It's a fast and easy procedure…"

She was mid-sentence when I put my shoes on and ran out the door without uttering a word to her. I'd never been so disrespectful in my life but I was in a daze.

The first thing I did was call Ted. I told him to meet outside his parents' house in 20 minutes because I was not going inside. I told him the news and he sat in the passenger seat tongue-tied. "Uh, what do we do now?" Clearly he was no help. I felt so alone and so afraid. I was completely opposed to abortion.

Almost immediately, I told my mom and a couple of my sisters, but nobody had a strong reaction either way. I didn't hear, "Oh no!" or "Congrats!" Having babies unwed before you're twenty years old is common in my family. I was confused about what to do. I didn't know if I would be able to go to college and make a life for myself outside of the trailer parks while raising a child. But, the one thing I did know was that having an abortion was a disgrace. I knew my mom and sister Joh had gotten assistance from WIC (Women, Infants, Children), the government nutrition program that helps low-income families afford formula and food, so I made an appointment. I had every intention of having this baby.

Which was kind of crazy because I had a boyfriend who was living with his parents and hiding the fact that we were even having sex, let alone having a baby. One night not long after I found out the news, we had sex and I saw blood on the mattress after. When I went to the bathroom, more blood came out into the toilet. I instantly thought I was having a miscarriage. I was more relieved than sad, thinking I wouldn't be pregnant anymore.

I went to the doctor and when they told me it was normal to bleed after sex when pregnant, it's hard for me to admit, but I was disappointed. I thought my nightmare was over. I knew deep down that Ted and I weren't ready for this. I also realized I was falling right into the same footsteps my mother took. I'd worked so hard to go the opposite direction of my upbringing—I was the first female to graduate high school in I don't know how many generations—and yet here I was. I did not want to be twenty-five with five kids, living on welfare, a man beating the shit out of me.

So I got an abortion. And it was a horrible experience in every way. Ted came with me to the clinic. When the doctor asked if a male student could be present during the procedure I just looked blankly. Ted said absolutely not. When she told him it was my decision and looked at me I just shrugged and said "sure." Ted did not like this. He kept being so loud and demanding. He was mad that there would be a man in the room when I was exposed and he wouldn't let it go. He was escorted outside before they did the procedure. So I lay there, by myself, hyperventilating, getting the baby sucked out of me. Crying, in agony, I felt worthless and irresponsible. I was the epitome of low-life trailer trash. I felt I deserved to suffer for what I'd done to this innocent life, and, at the same time, I knew if I had the baby, there'd be no way out for me. My sister Joh, who'd already given birth to her first baby, was stuck with a fiancé who beat her with pots and pans. (She eventually gained enough courage to be able to break free from this awful relationship she was stuck in.) I was desperately trying to break the chain.

After the abortion, I did not want to have sex with Ted again so I played the religion card. I told him I felt guilty that we had sex on Saturday nights and then went to church Sunday mornings. I insisted we stop having sex until we were married.

For God.

To my total shock, he agreed.

Honestly, Christianity saved me a few times during my childhood, and I credit it for teaching me good values. I always wanted to be good and sought out how to do that. When I was young and had no activities to do, I went to church with the lady who owned the trailer park because she offered a free ride. I met my best friend Elya in a youth group and she's still my best friend to this day. Later, with Ted, I went to church with his family during the lowest point of my life when my mom was off her rocker. She and my sister Joh, more and more a mini-me of my mom (thankfully, she caught on and bravely changed for the better later in life), hated that I was going so much, and they ganged up on me and accused me of being a hypocrite in a cult.

This was the only time in my life I ever thought about killing myself. I was trying to be a good person and it seemed like every direction I turned in life I failed. They broke me down, beat me up mentally so badly. I remember going into the bathroom bawling, locking the door, sitting on the toilet, and staring at razors in the drawer. But committing suicide is a sin so I didn't go through with it (nice, pick and choose your sins, Jamie). The other reason is that I knew my younger siblings desperately needed me.

After I graduated high school I had no clue that I could actually go to college. Nobody had ever gone before or knew how to help. Nobody knew about financial aid and scholarships and grants. After

I spent the first semester after high school depressed and in bed, feeling like a low life because all my friends were in college, my grandma surprised me with a "graduation gift" of $15,000 to go to college in Spain for one semester. I'd studied Spanish in high school and my mom and grandma thought it was a great idea for me to continue learning a second language. Random, I know, but hey, I wasn't complaining! My family had never been this proud of anyone, so I really felt like they believed in me so much. I couldn't believe my grandma was willing to take out a loan to make such a big investment in my future. When she handed me the "gift" of the check, she had tears in her eyes. "I'm so proud of you for graduating, Jamie." I was dumbfounded. I couldn't believe I'd made my grandma so proud!

I was woefully unprepared to go to Spain. I'd never been on an airplane. I'd only been out of the country once, when I drove six hours north to Toronto for a church retreat. In Spain I opted to stay with a host family. I wanted to experience a happy home but upon my arrival they asked if I was a fan of current president George W. Bush, and not knowing the right answer, I said "yes." It was all downhill from there.

Homesick, friendless and lonely, I dropped out after two months and came back upstate ashamed of myself. While I was away, things had gotten way worse for my siblings. My mom had been evicted yet again so while I was away she had moved into Hanshaw Trailer Park. She started disappearing up to Syracuse a lot. Guilt ridden, she usually came back home with bags of groceries. Suddenly she started vanishing and not bringing anything home. Taking matters into my own hands, I got a job as a waitress making pretty decent money, up to $100 per day in tips, at the BoatYard Grill. I even saved up enough money to buy a beater car. All of a sudden, I had a little cash and grubby hands got greedy. Mom told me I had to start paying her rent and my grandma suddenly insisted that Spain was a loan, not a gift, and demanded I pay her back. I couldn't believe it. How could she change it from a gift to a "loan"? I was only eighteen years old and could never afford to pay her that back. But I just got my grandma proud of me, I didn't want to lose her pride now. I began helping pay back the loan with her and my mom. There was no way I could pay back that loan just waitressing. Thank God Elya told me I could apply for financial aid and enroll at the local Tompkins Cortland Community College.

The situation at my mom's went into crisis mode. The trailer was a wreck—absolutely filthy, infested with mice. In mid-winter the heat and electricity were turned off. Usually my mom would go to the welfare office and get it turned back on but this time she didn't. Instead she put a kerosene heater in the living room and a loud, stinky generator in the bathroom. These things aren't safe to be inside your home but she said as long as we kept the door closed and the window open, it would get rid of all the dangerous fumes. Plus, there was a hole in the bathroom floor that allowed for extra ventilation. My siblings and I had to walk around with candles at night. The cupboards were bare and I realized my siblings were literally scrounging for food. I'd sneak them leftover bread and salad from the BoatYard whenever I could—and even got in trouble for it. I never felt like it was stealing though because it was stuff that would have been thrown away and it was delicious and hearty and necessary. Leah was so starving, she scraped mold off bread to make peanut butter and mayo sandwiches. You couldn't really taste the mold anyway. We were thankful that we even had bread because sometimes there would be none and we'd have to concoct a bologna and cheese roll-up. This is actually pretty tasty but the only problem is that it takes a lot of bologna and cheese roll-ups to feel full and we just never had enough for all of us. Fed up, I moved out of my mom's dump for good and rented my own tiny trailer for $250 per month. Which was super selfish of me, because my siblings were still stuck there. But I was just fending for myself, desperate to get away and make a better future for myself.

Months late on rent, Mom got evicted again not long after I moved—not a shocker—so she came over to my place and asked if my siblings could get off the school bus at my house. They literally had nowhere to go. I said yes and then Mom disappeared again. Little did I know, Mom had no intention of coming back to pick them up that night or anytime soon. It was days before she came back and when she did it was to ask for gas money, not because she'd found a home for my siblings to live in. I was terrified that CPS and the foster care system would get wind that she was MIA, take my siblings away and split them up. I was only nineteen years old the first time I began taking care of my little siblings AmyLynn and twins Leah and Dale.

My brother slept on the couch, my sisters in the spare room and I had my own bedroom (that wasn't very nice of me!). We all got along great at first and had a whole system worked out. The heat was never turned up past 55 degrees, the lowest it could go without the pipes freezing, because we couldn't afford it. But at least it was never turned off. If my brother complained about being cold I'd tell him to go put another sweatshirt on. We'd wrap ourselves in blankets or huddle together to stay warm. We all had our own jobs to do. Leah would help me keep the house clean. Because I was in school full-time, working part-time and also cheerleading, AmyLynn would watch the twins for me after school. And she got her first part-time job at McDonald's too. I told her if she wanted cable she'd have to pay for it because it was a luxury we couldn't afford. And so she did with her paycheck. The four of us spent Thanksgiving and Christmas mornings together alone and it really felt like a cohesive family unit for the first time in all of our lives, no matter how dysfunctional it might sound to anybody else.

But I knew I needed to make more money so I could support my siblings and me. I went to the career counselor in college and said, "Is there any degree I can get from a two-year college that will pay more than minimum wage?" She gave me a career test. I ranked highest for "teacher" or "nurse." I never wanted to be a nurse, I would have preferred teacher. But I couldn't afford to go to school another four years in order to get my teaching degree—I knew the BoatYard wouldn't let me get away with taking leftover family meals home to them much longer. So, I asked the counselor about nursing school. She said it was faster than a teaching degree but more rigorous, and had a wait list a mile long. Few made it in and only half actually survived the whole course. I didn't let those statistics deter me. I needed this job. I wrote a killer essay explaining how it was just my siblings and me living together relying on each other and how committed I was to doing well in this program so I could not only take care of patients but also my family.

I got into nursing school and it was life changing. Once I was away from my old life, I started to see the situation with clearer eyes. I learned so much about psychology and mental illness in my classes and I started diagnosing everyone in my life, including me. Such a typical nursing student! Being ditched by my mom and left with friends, guys, alone, I recognized I was codependent on my sisters. Like, if they did not NEED ME I felt awful. And I discovered that my mom was definitely a narcissist but possibly also mentally ill. It was the first time I actually felt bad for my mom rather than just hate her for choosing her drug friends over us. This didn't make it any less painful though.

My mom reappeared again and, weirdly, I got the feeling she expected to be taken care of by me. She demanded I give her money for the gas it took to come over with food (that she got from the free food pantry) for the kids. But the worst was when she tricked me.

She stopped into my job and told me the twins needed $100 each for a school trip. What school trip costs $100? I was so stupid, naïvely I handed over the money. The next day I asked Leah about the trip and she said, "What are you talking about? I never even wanted to go on that trip." My mom duped me. God only knows what she spent the money on.

When I confronted her about it, my mom punished me for yelling at her the best way she knew how—she took the kids away from me. With no legal custody, I had to let them go. My mom moved them into her new boyfriend's trailer, which was the most disgusting and dangerous place they'd ever lived. It had mice and bugs, and greasy motorcycle parts all over the floor and counters. It was filled with boxes and trash—there was nowhere to even sit down. We never lived in a mansion so that didn't really matter. What did matter was that this boyfriend violently grabbed my brother by the neck and, worst of all, molested my little sister.

They were living in a dangerous place and spinning out of control with no parental guidance. Leah was dating an older man in jail for pedophilia and Dale stole a lawnmower and drove it into town. That's when the cops finally and thankfully caught on to what was going on with our family. They busted him on the lawnmower and escorted him back to the trailer. What they found was a house of horrors with zero adult supervision. Of course my mom was nowhere to be found.

I was working at the restaurant when I got a voicemail from the police. They said they had my siblings in custody and would transfer them to foster care, unless an adult family member could take care of them. At this point I was living in a studio apartment the size of a small college dorm. They couldn't all sleep on my pull-out couch, so I attempted to buy a trailer that we could all live in. At first I was dejected because I was rejected by every bank. After running a credit check I figured out why. Turns out, my mom put a cellphone bill in my name and, naturally, let it go delinquent. Luckily, the owners of the trailer park had seen me around my whole life and knew I was good for it. "She pays her bills," one of the guys said. "She's really reliable."

I devised a handwritten contract to show them how I could pay it off with student loans and monthly payments. They let me pay $325 per month with an additional $2,000 payment (the amount I was allowed for student loans) at the beginning of each new semester for a three-bedroom trailer that was the nicest place we ever lived. The roof didn't leak and all the windows had screens, but it did have a hole in the floor. Trailers are notorious for having weak floors with holes.

"Are you gonna fix the hole before we move in?" I asked.

"Nope."

"Okay!"

Who was I kidding? I had no choice.

After multiple court appointments it became evident that my mom wasn't able to prove to the judge she could keep a job and provide a home for my younger siblings. At twenty years old the judge granted legal custody of my little sisters AmyLynn & Leah to me. (Leah chose to live with Joh at first.) Joh was granted legal custody of Dale. So the kids ended up separated, but at least all of us siblings were still together and no one ended up in foster care. Leah switched on and off living with me and Joh, who was much more lenient when she caught her smoking cigarettes.

My house, my rules.

These kids, now teenagers, had been running wild their whole lives and weren't happy with my strict ways. I was really hard on them on purpose because I wanted to be a good role model. I made them do chores and homework and get to the school bus on time. If they didn't, they'd hear from me about it for a week. I got really angry with them if they didn't get good grades. There was no smoking and no one of the opposite sex allowed in their bedrooms with the door closed. When AmyLynn had her boyfriend over she decided she was going to sit in between his legs while flirting and holding hands. I told her that she needed to get up and sit next to him because the way they were sitting was inappropriate. She said, "Why? You do it." I told her I was older than her and those were my rules. She looked at me incredulously. I am only three years older than her. This makes it difficult to enforce rules with "because I said so and I'm the adult" reasoning. But I did it anyway.

They hated me.

But in return, I tried to give them the love, attention, structure—and material things—we'd never had. I went to Leah's softball games and AmyLynn's musical. I bought them anything I could afford, to the point that AmyLynn got a little spoiled and expected it! I even treated myself to (discount) Abercrombie jeans. I was learning to take care of myself and my needs, too. I'd been dying to compete in the Miss New York USA pageant and had signed up for information on the website but never followed through. I'd never had time to do it or had the money for the dresses and hair and makeup. By this time, I had read a book titled *They Cage the Animals At Night* by Jennings Michael Burch and it ignited a passion in me to help more children who were orphaned by their parents. Since there were no orphanages I could volunteer at I began taking foster parenting classes. I'm pretty sure I'm the youngest person to ever graduate from those classes and begin taking children in. I was just twenty-two years old when I began taking care of my first foster child. She was a sixteen-year-old girl. Since I had a house filled with three teenagers I decided I deserved to take a weekend for myself. When I got a pamphlet inviting me to compete, I allowed myself to take a chance and go have some fun for a weekend. My best friend Elya watched the kids and it was a blast. It was the first time in I don't even know how long I was able to be a kid. I was green but ended up winning Miss Congeniality like Sandra Bullock and I was hooked. It gave me a sense of pride and self worth.

Just because I had such a great time, taking one weekend out for myself, didn't make me dread going back home to take care of my siblings and my foster child. I loved taking care of them and playing the mother role. I took tons of pictures and videos, to the point of being annoying, because my siblings and I had barely any photos at all up to that point in our lives. I had almost no baby pictures but somehow AmyLynn got a lot. There was no rhyme or reason.

I never took them to Chuck E. Cheese but I tried throwing them real birthday parties. Like at the bowling alley. My mom always let us have birthday parties but sometimes they weren't the type of "party" you'd expect. For my fifth grade birthday party my mom wasn't even there. She dropped my friends and me off and we spent the whole time cleaning the house because we'd been evicted yet again and had to get out before the end of the month.

My mom was invited to all the parties I threw for my siblings but usually didn't show up, didn't call or message in any way. She wasn't completely unaware of her hurtful ways. Eventually she would feel bad for failing to show up or just altogether forgetting, but instead of apologizing she would give a story about her car breaking down, not having gas, or some other lame excuse. Anything to make us feel sorry for her rather than be mad at her.

But at the twins' eighteenth birthday party I never expected this behavior from her. I got a call that day from the police that she'd left a suicide note and disappeared without a trace. They couldn't find her. On one hand, I was super scared she'd killed herself. On the other hand, I also knew she was weirdly desperate for attention. I had a hunch this was a sick game she was playing to steal the spotlight away from the twins. And make us once again just feel bad for her. I kept the disturbing news I'd received secret and the party went on as planned. The cops eventually found Mom and admitted her to the psych ward because she was "hearing voices. Sometimes they're good and sometimes they're bad," she told me. This was more than sad. This was scary. I'd never heard her say she heard voices before. What had these drugs done to my Momma?

Now, imagine going through all of this madness and, at the same time, trying to keep a twenty-year-old, sex-starved boyfriend happy. Ted was likely cheating behind my back and admitted to popping pills when I found them in his pocket, after he called them "candy." He was mopey and bitter about the time and attention I gave to my siblings. Even though I barely had time to do anything other than work, go to school and be a single parent to feral children, he got increasingly possessive and jealous and controlling. He was convinced I was cheating on him, which shows just how little he knew me. I didn't feel comfortable having sex with him—who I thought God had made my soul mate—so there was no way on earth I'd want to have sex with some random stranger.

We started fighting a lot and it escalated quickly. Because Ted didn't outright punch me the way my stepdad belted my mom, I didn't think he was abusive. But he was. He'd lock me in the bathroom for hours, until he decided he was done talking to me. If I didn't want to see him, he followed me. One time he stood outside my college class and stared at me through the window the entire hour. It took his brother-in-law coming into the school and physically escorting him out before he would leave. He broke into my house several times. One time I woke up startled from a dead sleep to find him cuddling into me. I was terrified because I didn't know what he was capable of or what he was thinking. I was also freaked out because I don't know how long he was there? How did I not wake up right when he came in? It was so insane that I actually thought he might kill me. I threatened to call the police and thankfully he left. Another time he busted down my door with his shoulder, ripping my phone out of my hands and screaming at me. This happened in front of AmyLynn, and I was not only scared he would hurt us, I was so embarrassed because once again, I wanted to be a role model but felt like I was following in my mom's footsteps.

I became so terrified of Ted, I asked a cute construction worker who sat next to me in class—fake name: Burt—to install a new front door lock and a chain lock on my bedroom door so I wouldn't find Ted wrapped around me in bed again. Nothing was more attractive to me than a man who could protect me. I started seeing him a lot. Ted did not like that I was seeing Burt. He would sit in his car watching my house waiting for Burt to leave. One morning, after he left, I went to pee. As I was sitting on the toilet I heard my front door rattling. The girls were at school so I knew it must be Ted. Scared shitless, I didn't even get a chance to wipe before I bolted off the toilet and ran with my panties around my ankles to my bedroom door, where I put the chain on just in the nick of time. Like in a horror movie, Ted reached his arm through the small crack the chain allowed and tried to grab me.

"I just want to talk to you!" he cried like a maniac.

I'd always threatened to call the cops (learned that trick from my Momma) and that was usually enough to get him to leave. This time he wasn't leaving so I actually called. But by the time they got there, Ted was gone. When the police went to question him, his mother lied and said he was with her the whole time.

Turns out, I wasn't much safer with Burt, who liked to get his shotgun out when he was drunk and high. "That guy's talking about my sister!" he slurred menacingly. No thanks. He went absolutely nuts when I dumped him. I tried to drive away, but he jumped in my backseat and refused to get out. Raise your hand if you've ever had a guy do this to you. It's scary and you feel utterly powerless, right? This guy sobbed and shouted, "But I love you!" until I threatened to call the police.

Considering my upbringing, I'm not sure how I knew these guys weren't husband material. In my world, if they didn't leave a bruise on my face or hold a gun to my head, you were doing good. It took going to nursing school to realize that just because they didn't beat me didn't mean they weren't being abusive.

I had always been the black sheep of the family, always trying so hard to be an upstanding person, but I came so close to falling into the same bitter cycle my mom was in. By my early twenties, I'd had an abortion, was taking care of three children, had vicious fights with boyfriends in front of them and used food stamps to put food on the table. But I had this weird way of recognizing it. My older sister Joh also began taking the steps my mother took by dropping out of high school and almost immediately having a baby out of wedlock with a man who she "loved" while he beat her to a pulp. She didn't give a damn what anyone thought though, as long as this man didn't make her a single mother raising a fatherless child.

The biggest difference between Joh and me? Somehow I always knew the way we lived our life was embarrassing and shameful. She never gave a crap. Did my DNA make a difference? Was this my father's greatest influence? I want to believe whoever my dad is, he must be pretty intelligent and a good man. I don't want to believe that I was conceived solely because he took advantage of my mom the night she "blacked out." I'll probably never know the truth about my dad or the night I was conceived.

The one thing I knew for sure from the beginning was that I yearned for a better life and a kind, intelligent man to be my husband. The problem was, I didn't think I deserved it and I didn't think a man like that actually existed anywhere other than in *The Notebook*.

At this point, I was at rock bottom. I had zero self-respect or self-worth. And I was emotionally exhausted.

That all changed when I met Stan.

Stan was a musician whose band played the local dive bar scene. He was considered a bit of a rock star in our neck of the woods, a big fish in a small pond. I friended him on Facebook because it'd always been my dream to be a singer and I had been taking singing lessons from my sister's chorus teacher. His band was the best-known band in the area. He was well on his way to becoming a Grammy-nominated musician and I wanted advice from a professional musician. Wink wink.

"Don't mess with him," my friends warned me. "He's the typical rock star, he sleeps around. Plus, he is eighteen years older than you!"

I messaged him anyway, he was so hot. Wink wink again. When he responded, I was impressed that he wrote eloquently and used correct grammar. I was used to the communication of immature boys, usually limited to, "Wut up?" or "Wat u doin?"

I liked that he was so much older because I craved maturity and stability. I did worry about his reputation. I'm glad I didn't listen to my friends, though, and made my own judgment. He wasn't a womanizer; he was more of a gentleman than anyone I've ever met. Often when you live life in the spotlight you get pegged as being whatever the rumors are about you—whether they're true or not. We went out for two months before we had our first kiss, and he was the first guy I dated who made me feel safe, never pressured. When I had to stop in the middle of having sex, he never got mad. For the first time in my life, I didn't feel like I was being used. Sex felt like a loving act. It was a major epiphany. When I put the brakes on while having sex, he just rolled over, wrapped his arms around me, and said, "It's okay." Then he kissed me good night. No questions asked. That was true love.

Stan was the best thing that ever happened to me. He helped me change my old ways of negative thinking in so many positive ways. When I tried to pick fights with him, because it was ingrained in me that it was impossible to be happy all day long in a relationship, he wouldn't let me. He was so different than the numbskulls I'd dated before. He didn't do drugs, we didn't have to get sloshed every time we went out, and he was the polar opposite of possessive and controlling. Maybe to a fault. We were so loosey-goosey, we were never officially a couple. He encouraged me to spread my wings and get the hell out of Dodge, especially since by now the twins were old enough to take care of themselves and I had helped my foster child be placed in her forever home.

Stan, and college, opened my eyes to the fact that there was life outside of the trailer parks.

After nursing school I immediately got a job as an RN and saved up $6,000 for a new car. My beater Ford Escort was a rust bucket with over 200,000 miles on it but that bad boy still ran. I couldn't imagine just dumping it for a new car. Instead I decided to do something else for myself with the money I saved. I enrolled in Berklee College of Music's summer vocal program in Boston because I wanted a voice like Carrie Underwood.

By now twenty-three, I was the oldest student there. Most were high school kids, but I had the best summer of my life, even if I regressed a little bit. I was hanging out with kids basically because there was nobody there my age. This is something I would have loved to do as a child but never was able to. So what if I became BFF 4EVER with eighteen-year-olds for the summer!

I was a little out of my league at Berklee—not quite as bad as those clueless people humiliating themselves during *American Idol* auditions but nowhere near ready to record "Smoke Break." By the way, I was one of those clueless people. I auditioned for *AI* in Philadelphia at the Eagles' football stadium. After sitting there for 10 hours, next to people dressed like Batman and the Bride of Chucky, I didn't get a chance to sing for Simon or Paula or Randy. I stood in front of one of about 50 random judges and got 10 seconds to belt "Settlin'" by Sugarland before I got the raised hand that shushed me and sent me to the reject pile. No golden ticket for me, but Elya and my little sissies congratulated me anyway with a bouquet of flowers.

Back to Berklee. It was sort of random that I was there but that's when fate stepped in. My roommate was obsessed with *The Bachelorette*. I'd never seen it, we didn't have cable at the trailers growing up, but of course I'd heard of it. I mean, everyone's heard of *The Bachelor*. It was Ali Fedotowsky's season and I fell in love with her and the show. Some people watch *The Bachelor* ironically, to laugh at it and make fun of it all, but I was a true believer. I thought it was real and bought into the fairy-tale romance hook, line, and sinker.

So when the commercial came on and said, "If you'd like to date our next Bachelor..." I had hearts in my eyes and butterflies in my stomach. I dreamed of a handsome prince whisking me away from my dismal life, like Cinderella. Naïve, I know. I applied immediately.

I was so clueless about how the show worked, I thought I was applying to be on *The Bachelorette*. I didn't know almost all of them had appeared on *The Bachelor* first, and then, if rejected by the Bachelor but beloved by fans, were luckily chosen to be Bachelorette. You'd have better luck being struck by lightning. Nevertheless, I pulled out all the stops to get on the show. I sent in a picture in my best red dress and said I was proud to be a successful registered nurse, though I'd only just graduated nursing school and worked in a hospital less than a year. I went with it anyway. And I spoke about my proudest achievement in life, the ability to raise my younger siblings.

I never thought they'd pick me in a million years. But six months after I applied, I got the call. I was headed to finals weekend in Los Angeles. Producers sequester you in a hotel, take away your cellphone and grill you for two days to make sure you're not an axe murderer. You answer endless questionnaires, meet with a private investigator and a psychologist. I thought for sure when producers found out about the extreme trailer-trashiness of my childhood I'd be sent packing. I had no idea this was the type of show that thrived on pity-me-my-life's-been-so-hard drama. They ate my story right up. My nightmare apparently made great TV.

When I was chosen to be on season 16—which starred floppy-haired winemaker Ben Flajnik—I was beyond excited but also shocked. I thought they'd made a terrible mistake. This was an iconic show. I wasn't a model. I wasn't rich. I didn't come from a good family. I was honest about everything and they still chose me. I told them I'd only seen one episode of *The Bachelor* and they sent me DVDs of Brad Womack's season to get up to speed. I had no idea that *The Bachelorette*, a dozen mostly nice guys competing for one woman, was a completely different animal than *The Bachelor*, two dozen catty women scratching each other's eyes out for one man.

The show's most famous producer, Elan Gale (creator of viral Instagram accounts "Tinder Nightmares" and "Texts From Your Ex"), flew to upstate New York to film my at-home package. I was a nervous wreck beforehand, terrified that once he saw my trailer, he'd change his mind. To not appear so poor, I vacuumed and cleaned my house like a maniac, and even though one of my neighbors' yard looked like an episode of *Hoarders*, they helped me plant pretty flowers in my front yard. I even put out tea and donuts.

Elan had hired a local film crew and when they finally found the trailer park (it wasn't on the GPS), they were cranky and annoyed. Because the show was filmed secretly they didn't know what they were there for. Elan, as fans of the show know, looks like he just crawled out of a ditch: a homeless hipster with wild hair and beard. I had hot rollers in my hair, because I thought large, bouncy curls were THE style, but the crew looked at me with total disgust. I was obviously trailer trash. But Elan got what he wanted after a lot of coaxing: Me telling my sob story, teary-eyed.

Everyone was so excited that I was leaving to be on *The Bachelor*. Except my mom. She had no idea because I couldn't get ahold of her. Even Stan was supportive. The nurses on my floor were diehard fans and gave me great advice: Don't be catty, needy or desperate. I was told to bring nine gowns for rose ceremonies, but I didn't own nine gowns and I couldn't afford to buy all new dresses. So I brought all my pageant gowns from the secondhand store. The only new things I bought were sandals and shorts.

Before I stepped foot in the mansion, I genuinely believed I could meet my husband and live happily ever after. But the second I sat in that limo heading to meet the Bachelor, it was over for me. I was instantly insecure and knew I didn't belong there. "Go back to the trailer park, where you belong!" kept running through my head. Kacie "B" Boguskie was in my limo and I was so intimidated by her beauty and confidence, I could barely speak. Why would Ben pick someone like me, when he could be with Kacie, who wasn't trailer trash and probably had a father and money and a nice house? The first night, when the drop-dead gorgeous girls, including Courtney Robertson, Casey Shteamer and Rachel Trueheart, fought for Ben's attention, I talked to the grandma who was brought in for comic relief. I did not feel nearly as incredible as the other women there. I felt like I had more in common with the grandma than I did with any of these women.

Unlike self-assured "VIP cocktail waitress" Blakely Shea, I was so embarrassed about where I came from, I didn't want to be found out. Ben was sophisticated and smart (eventual winner Courtney would call him a "snob" in her *New York Times* bestselling book *I Didn't Come Here to Make Friends*), so when he pulled me aside during our first trip in Sonoma, I told him I didn't want a one-on-one date and not to pick me. With an attitude like that, I take full blame that I barely got any airtime and I only lasted seven episodes.

And the seven episodes I made it through were torture for me. I had zero friends—I was the unpopular outsider who never found a clique. I was scared and anxious and lonely. Ben barely knew I was alive and even the producers started giving up on me. I'd never been a quitter so, as Courtney would say, I pulled on my big girl panties and decided to try hard one last time to capture Ben's heart. Chris Harrison encouraged me to "open up" and in *Bachelor* terms that meant two things.

1. *Open up about something traumatic.* I think the only reason I was kept around for seven episodes wasn't because Ben liked me. We barely spoke five words. Elan wanted me to "open up" about my past but I really didn't feel comfortable talking to Ben about my "impoverished, abusive upbringing." I was embarrassed and it didn't seem like a good way to win a man's heart. Besides, I barely knew Ben, let alone trusted and respected him enough to share my most intimate, less-than-flattering life story. He seemed like a very judgmental, un-empathetic guy. When we were in Panama, we visited a poor local village and hung out with the natives. It was cold and rainy that day, and we all infamously wore skimpy bikinis adorned with beautiful beads made by the tribal women (Ben wore a loincloth with nothing underneath). Well, all the ladies were cold and miserable but sucking it up. I'll never forget what Ben said right in front of these wonderful people, as we ate cold sandwiches in one of their huts, which had no indoor plumbing. "I can't wait to get back to the hotel and take a hot shower and have a warm meal," he moaned. I was totally grossed out and he became so unattractive, I didn't care about getting a rose. "I like these cold sandwiches," I shot back.

2. *Do something sexual.* Ben had already made out with everyone in our house, except for me. As we all know by now, this would be difficult because I was still the most awkward person on the planet sexually. But I wasn't a quitter and Ben didn't deserve Option No. 1 so I decided to go with Option No. 2.

About two weeks before Hometown Dates, I knew it was sink or swim time (insider skinny-dipping reference alert!). I had one last chance to win this guy over. Now, this is going to sound like an excuse, but there's a strong possibility I intentionally sabotaged myself. As Hometowns got closer, I got more and more freaked out about bringing Ben back to upstate New York. There was no freakin' way that was happening. Can you picture Ben Flajnik meeting my mother and whatever dentally-challenged dude she was dating at that moment? Would my mother be high as a kite? Would she even show up? On the other hand, I wanted to protect my family from Ben's and *Bachelor* fans' judgment. I didn't want to cause my siblings pain. The thought of all this kept me up at night.

So here's what happened, though I'm sure many of you already know. At my final rose ceremony, in a last ditch act of desperation—my fellow nurses warned me!—I attempted to make out with Ben and it ended up topping every "most cringe-worthy moments in *Bachelor* history" list until Juan Pablo showed up. Which is saying a lot.

Before he pulled me aside, I downed a couple vodka sodas in the bathroom for liquid courage. Then I found him and grabbed his hand like I was some sort of seductress.

"I have a big surprise for you," I cooed.

"You do?" Ben said.

"Do you like surprises?"

"Uh huh."

"Good!"

"I want to turn Ben on," I lied in my voiceover. "I want him to be attracted to me and I will be aggressive. He better brace himself because he's gonna be shocked."

I apologized to Ben for not showing him how I felt about him up to this point.

"I think about you often," I lied again. "I think about things I'd like to do with you."

Ben opened his eyes wide and raised his eyebrows.

"Oh?"

"I had really big plans. Do you want me to show you?"

I then proceeded to get up and straddle Ben like in a lap dance, only it looked more like I was getting on a horse, and nearly ripped my pageant dress. I was buzzed.

"I don't get fancy with anyone unless I really want to," I said.

"This is fancy?" a perplexed Ben said.

"I would like to get a little fancier, but this will work for now."

By the way, "fancy" did not go viral as a new synonym for horny. It hasn't made the Urban Dictionary or anything. Oy, I still blush reliving this scenario in my head. I was trying so hard to be sexy but I was just plain awkward.

I leaned in for a passionate kiss but started laughing as soon as our mouths met.

"You can't keep laughing when I try to make out with you," Ben said, annoyed.

I got off his lap like a linebacker who just tackled the quarter-back and, after a short discussion about how awkward our kiss was, we decided to give it one more college try.

"When my mouth was open, your mouth was closed and vice versa," I scolded him.

"So do you want my mouth closed or open?"

"First it's going to be closed and then we'll feel each other out," I instructed. "Once we feel each other out, we're gonna open our mouths."

Ben scratched his face uncomfortably.

"That's normally how kissing goes. You're not the first woman I've kissed."

We made out again and he still didn't keep his mouth shut. He just came at me with a wide-open mouth ready to stick his tongue down my throat. This time I couldn't keep my mouth shut.

"Mouth closed!" I directed. "Mouth open! Now we're going to explore…"

"I can't handle this right now!" Ben freaked out and backed out. We were done and we hadn't even started. O.V.E.R. and get out.

I was sent packing at the rose ceremony. I could tell Ben was going to let me do the walk of shame solo so I put him on the spot. "Aren't you going to walk me out?" It was the least he could do after sticking his tongue in my mouth the wrong way!

"Oh, right." As he led me out, I gave him a tip. "Give Nicki a chance." He ignored my instructions. Again.

The Bachelor was a terrible experience for me in the moment but it took hindsight for me to appreciate what a gift it was. I wasn't just trailer trash, I was special. They chose *ME* from thousands of women to join "*Bachelor* Nation." So many women would chop off their left arms to be a part of *The Bachelor*, but I got the once in a lifetime opportunity. It also showed me that I was capable of anything and was not limited by my background. I'd never let it hold me back again.

As soon as I got my cellphone back from the producers, I called my sisters to get a ride home after the nine-hour flight back from Panama City. I was hung over, and exhausted and stressed-out from trying to hide the real me for the last four weeks. I needed unconditional love from my family, the people who knew and appreciated the real me. None of them answered their phones.

I called Stan. Even though he was hunting in the woods, he answered and then he dropped everything to pick me up at the airport. When I got in the car, he leaned over and kissed me. Unlike Ben, it was normal and natural.

I felt safe.

I felt wanted.

I cried.

CHAPTER 3

Bride-To-Be...Or Not-To-Be?

Like a pig in mud, I was happy. Stan and I were unofficially together. The sex was the best I'd ever had—our chemistry was off the charts—but we were allergic to labels. We allowed each other a lot of space and independence and avoided calling each other boyfriend or girlfriend. At the same time, I returned to my first job at Cortland Regional Medical Center as a labor and delivery nurse and started making real money for the first time in my life. My younger siblings, now 20 and 18, were old enough to take care of themselves and doing pretty well, despite what they'd been through. AmyLynn was following in my footsteps at Tompkins Cortland Community

College. Dale began working in construction and Leah was pregnant with her first child.

And, again like a pig in mud I was stuck. The *Bachelor* experience had opened up my world irreversibly. I now had evidence that there was so much more to life, and felt claustrophobic and trapped upstate. Like so many young, idealistic dreamers, visions of New York City danced in my head. After *The Bachelor*, I'd been hired for a couple of hosting gigs and event appearances in Manhattan and was energized. I fell in love with TV hosting. Like Ol' Blue Eyes always said, "If you can make it there, you'll make it anywhere." I no longer felt crappy about myself. For the first time in my life, I believed in myself and I wanted that challenge. I wanted to be the most successful person ever to make it out of the Beacon View trailer park. If I stayed any longer, I'd feel like a failure. Stan, God love him, understood my yearning. He knew that I wouldn't and couldn't just get married and pop out babies. "You do you," he told me. So I paid off my trailer, and paid it forward and put another family in it, which made me feel so proud and free. I packed up Stan's truck, and moved to New York City with his blessing and $5,000. "Pay me back when you can," he said. Nobody had ever done anything like that for me. Burned by Grandma, I should have been skeptical, but I knew Stan meant it.

Within a month, I got a call from the producers of *Bachelor Pad 3*, the original *Bachelor* spin-off where *Bachelor* Nation rejects scratched each other's eyes out, while boning, for $250,000. Reality was biting in NYC and I hadn't gotten a job yet. Unlike *The Bachelor*, which didn't pay diddly-squat, this show paid about $1,500 for every episode until I was eliminated, so I had no reason not to do it. Plus, c'mon people, it was a possible $250,000 prize! I ran it by Stan, who was completely supportive again. "Go ahead! Do your thing," he told me. He was a little *too* supportive, considering this was also a show meant for very attractive alumni to hook up and possibly fall in love, no matter how ridiculous the circumstances. Stan wasn't even slightly jealous, which was good and bad. Partly out of spite, I said, "YES" to *Bachelor Pad*. And if I met someone I liked, I was going to give it a shot.

My self-esteem was way healthier than when I was on *The Bachelor* but all that progress got tossed out the window as soon as I arrived at the mansion in Los Angeles. *Bachelor Pad* was even cliquier than *The Bachelor*, and despite having Rachel Truehart, Jaclyn Swartz and Blakeley Shea from my season as a no-brainer squad, I was relegated to weirdo loner status again. This particular season they cast random "Super Fans" on the show but they were completely ostracized and ignored by the "real" *Bachelor* people. Of course, they became my best friends there.

Because I have a vagina and boobs, there was some interest in me from the guys, who included sweetheart Nick Peterson (still love him to this day), Ed Swiderski and Kalon McMahon (totally shady dudes), fan fave Michael Stagliano (pretended to be sweet but a player, imo), and drum roll please, Chris Bukowski. Again, I barely watched the show so I had no clue who Chris was. He'd apparently just been eliminated from Emily Maynard's *Bachelorette* season, everybody felt sorry for him and he was still in good graces with *Bachelor* fans. The buzz in the mansion was all CHRIS! CHRIS! CHRIS!—he was the newest, biggest *Bachelor* "star" at the house. The cool, hot guy every girl wanted.

"Oh my God, he looks like Gerard Butler!" Blakeley squealed. I didn't think so at all and wasn't attracted to Chris even slightly. I was so out of the loop, I was actually hoping Brad Womack would show up. I didn't know he was the biggest jerk ever in the history of *The Bachelor*, (until Juan Pablo came along). I saw like one scene of him wanting to commit to Emily and thought he was a romantic prince. Hah! I was so disappointed in the guy choices I had on *Bachelor Pad*, I remember being in an early ITM (In the Moment) interview and whining, "Is this it?"

With my options limited and mob mentality seeping into my brain, I quickly found myself wanting Chris Bukowski, too. Bad. The deal was sealed when he stared at me with those hypnotic, translucent blue eyes and said, "My mom and my sister are your biggest fans. They were hoping you'd be here."

I was thinking, "Umm, did they actually watch my season and see my kissing catastrophe with Ben?" Instead I should have been thinking, "He's probably using this line on every single girl here."

On *Bachelor Pad*, all the girls had to partner up with a guy and before Chris had a chance to ask me, 32-year-old virgin Ryan Hoag from DeAnna Pappas' season swooped in on me. I didn't want to be rude so I said, "Sure?" Just like that, like a question. Blakeley was the only woman left, so Chris was paired with her by default. She decided this meant they were also paired up romantically but Chris wasn't into the VIP waitress because she was too batshit crazy for him. So to prevent a rabbit from being boiled on the stove or something *Fatal Attraction*-ey like that, Chris and I had what I thought was a secret relationship behind Blakeley's back.

I was the only one in the dark, by the way. Our secret smiles and flirtations were hot to me but it wasn't enough for this horny little boy disguised as a man. We finally got some alone time in what was known as the "Bumper Room," the only room with only one bed in it. The other rooms were filled with bunk beds. This made it the perfect spot for hookups. Chris and I ended up there after a night of drinking.

"I'm not wearing anything under the blanket," he whispered to me.

"It's not happening," I whispered back.

There was no way I was going to do anything other than kiss Chris with a million cameras and microphones on us.

My hard NO did not go well with his hard-ON. The second he realized I was a prude who wouldn't even go to second base, I was dunzo. The next morning Chris got a date card, but he picked Sarah Newlon, a sure thing who'd already slept with two other guys there, according to rumors rampant in the house. While they steamed up a hot tub at a nearby Hilton, I waited up all night for him, like a doofus.

I was so oblivious, one of the female producers later admitted she was dying to tell me to go to bed to save me further humiliation.

I had no idea that Chris was having a full-on fling with Sarah and saying despicable and disrespectful things about me in his interviews, like I was "desperate and a yapper. I feel like the only way to shut her up is to kiss her. But there's just no spark there. I just look at her boobs." (I'm still a "yapper" but not so desperate anymore!). This boob also compared me to a used car he traded in for a new car (Sarah). "You get the nice new car smell," he said, "and this is so much smoother and nicer for me." His mom and sister must have been so proud.

Spoiler alert, I didn't win $250,000. Four episodes in, I got eliminated from the show. It took everything in me to stand up for myself, but on the way out the door I called out Chris for his boorish behavior and warned him he'd regret it one day. Flash-forward three years and, after acting like a complete "toolbag" (his words, not mine) on subsequent *Bachelor* and *Bachelor in Paradise* shows, Chris made a formal apology on *After Paradise* to all the women he treated badly and announced his retirement from reality TV. He admitted his quest for fame "completely ruined me, my family and my career."

That apology was too little, too late for me. I'm such a bad grudge holder, not the best characteristic, I know. I forgive him but I'll never forget the way he treated me. My experience on *Bachelor Pad 3* was a nightmare, largely due to Chris, and once again it was a huge relief to get away from all those people. But at least I got a new

BFF, Erica Rose, who traded in her tiara for the gavel she now wears around her neck (literally) after graduating law school. And this might surprise you, but I am still friends with a few of the producers from the show. Otherwise, I rarely had a good experience with anyone in *Bachelor* Nation, especially the guys, who I found particularly shady. Once, between my *Bachelor* and *Bachelor Pad* seasons, I went to a pool party in LA with a bunch of alumni and really hit it off with Ryan Park, the solar energy guy from Ashley Hebert's season. We hung out all day, laughing and talking and bonding, so I thought. But at the end of the night, when he drove me back to my hotel, I made it clear that I was not the kind of girl to sleep with a guy the same day I met him. His demeanor completely changed and he coldly dumped me off at the door and I never heard from him again. Guess he was exactly the kind of guy my Momma warned me about: just interested in getting in my pants. In other news, Andi Dorfman's ex-fiancè, Josh Murray, reached out to me while they were dating. I thought it was strange, considering it was on LinkedIn! We didn't really have any business to discuss. Good luck on that other reality show *Famously Single*, buddy!

With icky interactions like these, plus making a complete fool of myself for the second time on national television, I slunk back home and into Stan's arms, feeling like a friggin' idiot. As always, he had my back and made me feel better about myself, even as I heard about my hometown locals making fun of me. Stan's support was so unwavering, I never felt closer to him. He never once made me feel anything less than normal and desirable. When I'd spend too much time thinking about how silly and foolish I had been, he'd remind me of all the reasons why I was a great person. Sex with Stan was the way it was supposed to be with a lover—normal and healthy and safe and experimental. He was the one for me, and I didn't want to be in this shade of gray area with him anymore. We were head over heels for each other and for the first time in my life, I was all in. This was a big deal to me. We finally made our love official—I know this because we changed our status on Facebook to "in a relationship." Otherwise, it might have been hard to tell. We were very chill with each other about commitment and giving each other space. I was still living 200 miles away in New York City because when I got back from *Bachelor Pad*, I landed a job at Columbia University Medical Center. I'd work my tail off four nights in a row, so I could spend the next three with Stan. Because Stan had gigs pop up randomly, he had less flexibility than I did. So I'd work a full night shift from 7 pm to 7:30 am, give report of my patients and then head straight to the bus station. With no sleep I'd hop on a bus and go back and forth between the city and upstate every time we wanted to see each other.

If you've been in a long-distance relationship, you know what comes next. It's not rocket science. It wasn't working. This was way too hard. We had huge fights because I wanted to see him more, and it just wasn't possible. I refused to settle back home but Stan's entire life and livelihood were up there. He wasn't able to just up and move to New York City to be with me. One night, after a long shift, I made the mistake of calling him when I was exhausted and picked a fight. That phone conversation changed everything. With tears in my eyes and sorrow in my voice I told him I just can't do this anymore. I only saw him once a month for a few days. I wanted to be *with* someone. I wanted to go home every night to someone. I wanted to get married and have children. When would this happen for us? I didn't see a light at the end of the tunnel. I broke up with him, and true to his character, he didn't stop me. He didn't say, "Don't do this. Stay with me." He let me go, for good this time.

By now, the age of Tinder had dawned, and suddenly single in Manhattan, I started swiping left and right. My good friend Kirsten introduced me to this ego-boosting dating app. It was fun for about five minutes. Okay, maybe like 30 minutes. The worst date I went on was with Kirsten. We wanted to double date so the first guy who said he had a single friend with him we decided to meet up with. I swear this guy said he was in his late twenties but he couldn't have been far out of his teens. He didn't just look young, he acted like my little brother. His roomie was pretty young looking too. Their apartment was like walking into a dorm room—a really fancy dorm room with a view. Mommy and Daddy's money? I don't know. There was hardened pizza crust and empty beer cans laying all over. Kirsten and I stayed all of five minutes before we dashed out of there. We still laugh about that one. The "best" date I went on was with a standup comic. I took Erica Rose with me to make sure he wasn't a serial killer, and when I showed up with a friend in tow, he was a pretty good sport.

Because that was pretty psycho of me. Actually, I was the good sport because he'd posted a picture that made him look like a model and when we arrived he was at least 50 pounds heavier. I wasn't going to let him get away with that.

"Did you gain some weight?" I asked bluntly. "When did you take that picture? Ten years ago?"

Because he was a comic he could handle it. The three of us sat down for a drink and he was genuinely funny, busting us up with tales from his Tinder nightmares. Erica excused herself so we could get to know each other better but when she left it was like the record scratched. Suddenly, it was totally awkward and we had zero chemistry. The laughter died.

Okay, that was a little melodramatic. It wasn't that bad. And through Tinder, I actually met a Wall Street guy I sort of seriously dated because I was lonely. His name was Marco and he was loaded and had a huge apartment in Chelsea. He was the kind of guy who owned a $4,000 white couch, which was a sign to me that he might be a little OCD. He loved that couch, which I found strange because it's just an effin' couch. One night, he freaked the ef out when my puppy, Lady, got scared and peed on it. The meltdown over the couch wasn't a deal breaker in and of itself—I mean, I sort of understand, I guess, since my puppy peed on his couch! But it represented a much bigger problem. I realized I wasn't comfortable dating a really wealthy dude. Like Ben, I couldn't imagine bringing Marco home to meet my family. Guys with white couches and financial stability couldn't possibly understand where I came from or what I'd been through. If he was worried about his white couch getting dirty, I couldn't imagine taking him home to muck poo at my sister's little farm.

I always had one foot out the door with Marco. I always had one foot out the door with *every* guy I'd ever been with. My expectations had shot so sky high, I was certain I'd be alone forever. Who could meet my impossible standards? On the one hand, my nitpickiness had kept me from becoming promiscuous or settling with bad men. On the other hand, it kept me from being happy in *any* relationship. It bummed me out.

This was my mindset when I decided to take a chance on the unconventional way to find my happily ever after. (Understatement of the century.) I had nothing to lose so I was brutally honest while stating who I am and what I am looking for. What, or should I say who, I wanted was very simple but very specific:

- *A man—not a boy.*

- *From a big, stable, welcoming family.*

- *Wasn't too rich but had no debt.*

- *Didn't hate his job. Didn't care if he was a plumber or an accountant, as long as he was passionate about his work.*

- *I could feel safe and secure with. Would accept me and my family as is, baggage and all.*

It's strange choosing to go gung-ho and put your heart on your sleeve for a scientific-based marriage arranged by "experts." Part of me thought it could be the answer I've been looking for all along. But was I just tricking myself into wanting something seemingly "good"—kind of like how I tricked myself into wanting Chris Bukowski? How could I possibly marry a stranger? But like I said before, the truth was, after all I'd been through, I really craved the maternal babying the experts would provide. They'd hold my hand the whole way through and do everything in their power to help me hold on to everlasting love. I really felt like I didn't know how to be in a relationship without sabotaging it. I had trust and commitment issues. I liked the idea of having people I could trust guide me in my relationship. I knew I needed someone to flat out tell me when I'm being ridiculous or when I need to step up and not take certain treatment. I didn't really know how to differentiate the two. My dating history began with taking way too much crap and then when I realized I was being treated poorly (thank you nursing school) I went the complete opposite direction - if anyone gave me the slightest sign that they weren't treating me right or may not treat me right in the future I killed the relationship. No questions asked. I thought I was doing myself a favor. I didn't know how to find the happy medium.

I'd never admit it out loud, but I absolutely loved the idea of having experts help me in a relationship. When I left, I was more hopeful than nervous.

And when I found out that there was a match for me my mouth dropped open. I couldn't speak. One sentence kept running through my head.

I'm screwed.

The first person I wrote was Stan, because he was my best friend. Then I called my sisters because in precisely two weeks, they'd be bridesmaids in my *wedding*.

I called my mom. When I couldn't reach her I tried another number. I literally have five different numbers in my phone for my mom. Her number and location changed more than I could ever keep track of. When all numbers failed I just gave up. I never left messages because she was always using some random dude's phone. There's nothing weirder than calling the number your Mom gives you to get ahold of her and when you get to the voicemail a scruffy male's voice is on the other end.

In two weeks, I would be betrothed to a complete stranger. Most brides take like a year to plan their weddings. I didn't have that luxury. Fortunately or unfortunately, I didn't have time to be a Bridezilla, either. But a "perfect" wedding didn't really matter to me anyway. I was thinking all about my future husband and our connection. I wanted *that* to be perfect. I had been dying to be in a loving, stable relationship. One that I could count on lasting a lifetime. I desperately wanted to have someone to go home to every night and eat dinner together and talk about our future children. I could not care less about my wedding dress, the food or the flowers.

Most women take their mom wedding dress shopping with them but my mom didn't even know yet that I was getting married. My sisters and I still couldn't get ahold of her. Instead, I took my best friends. The dress I chose was literally 5 times too big, it was a size 10 and I wear a 2. It was simple and straightforward, mermaid cut on the bottom, sweetheart cut on top. I didn't feel comfortable getting a puffy or lacey gown that would make me look like the top of a wedding cake. I wanted to look über-attractive to my unknown groom. So I sewed in my Victoria's Secret Bombshell strapless bra to give me a double cup size and lots of cleavage.

I invited 25 guests but I was so scared that when I told my family and friends what I'd gotten myself into, they'd stage an intervention and check me into the loony bin. Then nobody would show up, including me. Most of them didn't even know what I had been up to in my love life. To my shock, almost everyone was supportive, including my mom, when I finally found her and told her. All she had to say was, "Honey, you're going to make a beautiful bride. And that man is going to be so lucky to have you as a wife." She didn't care if I went to Myrtle Beach with three dudes or got married to a complete stranger. It was all the same to her.

Funny story, I assumed there'd be enough room for 25 guests but there wasn't and I had to un-invite a few people. Oops, sorry again, Crissy! I only had one friend refuse my invitation. "Marriage is not a joke, Jamie," she sniped condescendingly (we are not friends anymore). I didn't invite my grandmother or grandfather, who called me a "cunt," "bitch," "liar," and "thief" publicly on Facebook while I was on *The Bachelor*. Later, my grandfather sent my new husband an email warning him about how terrible of a person I am. (More on this later.) With no older male in my life suitable to walk me down the aisle, I asked my younger brother Dale to be the man. He was honored.

It all happened so fast, I forgot that I was still sort of dating Marco, the rich guy, on and off. When I gave him the breaking news, he unexpectedly broke down in tears. "I love you so much!" he sobbed. "Please don't do this!" Whoa, I had no idea he felt this way about me. The only person who'd ever felt that strongly about me was Stan. I definitely couldn't invite him. Could I? My friends were on board with this whole thing but the one question they had for me was about Stan. Was it over for good?

"If it was meant to be, it would've been," I told them. "I'm going to give this a shot."

Do I even have to say that Stan was *fine* with me marrying a stranger? I've never said this publicly, but he actually helped me write my wedding song. (Gasp, I know!) I wanted our first dance to be monumental and I couldn't find an appropriate song that symbolized the marriage of two people who didn't know jack about each other. I didn't want to creep this guy out by being super lovey-dovey stalkerish too soon. I almost chose "At the Beginning" the love song from *Anastasia*, because the lyrics were spot on about starting a journey together. But ultimately I decided a Disney song was too cheesy.

In a panic, I grabbed a bottle of wine and invited a friend over to help me write an original song for my first dance with my future husband. I wanted the song to be intimate and friendly, and to mark the beginning of our journey together. But he flaked so Stan stepped in and saved the day. Here's what we wrote:

> *It seems so crazy but it's happening*
>
> *Now it all comes down to this*
>
> *We're exchanging vows, exchanging rings*
>
> *A journey born within a wish*
>
> *Here's to the firsts in life*
>
> *And here's to all that lies ahead*
>
> *To believing with all of our might*
>
> *Here's to this love experiment*
>
> *And now it all begins*
>
> *Here with our family and friends*
>
> *Right now it all begins*
>
> *This beautiful experience*
>
> *Taking the first of many steps*

The first of many memories

So lucky to be truly blessed

Yeah moments like this are what we dream

Here is to learning to fly

Sharing the tears and sentiments

To starting a brand-new life

Here's to this love experiment

And now it all begins

Here with our family and friends

Right now it all begins

This beautiful experience

And you try not to cry

As you look down the aisle to another

And then everyone smiles

While your hearts racing wild

That moment you discover

This is it…

And now it all begins

Here with our family and friends

Right now it all begins

This beautiful experience

It seems so crazy but it's happening

Yes, I know this is slightly insane. Possibly inappropriate. Definitely bizarre. But as I told my friends, Stan did not want to commit to me and start a life together. A complete stranger was willing to trust fate and marry me. He was already my hero—fearless and brave, in my mind.

Our wedding day was hectic, chaotic, and scary. Nothing lined up the way I wanted it to. When I put my wedding dress on it didn't zip. What?! It didn't zip?! Nope, I had to cut that bombshell bra out, which knocked out the chance of having any boobies. Gone was the idea I'd be steamy sexy for my stranger hubs. I went flat chested all the way. But God knows that was the least of my problems. I don't want to bore you with all the crazy details of our wedding day. To say it was a disaster is an understatement. Chances are you were one of the millions of people who watched on their TVs and got to witness that nightmare first-hand.

Let me just end on this note: Jamie Lynn Spears (yes, I love Britney and Jamie!) had just released her first country song titled "How Could I Want More" and after meeting my new, stranger hubby the lyrics were really dead on for me. Sounds corny, but this song helped me relax and reminded me to be thankful for my new husband, Doug Hehner.

Looking at a good man

Who ought to be the right guy

He's got that kinda heart that

Any girl would die for

So, how could I want more?

How could I want more?

CHAPTER 4

"A Vacation Where Two People Get To Know Each Other"

They say you really don't know someone until you travel with them. Well, I didn't know Jack about Doug, so I guess hopping on a plane immediately after getting hitched is a smart way to bond. Or insane. Either way. I think it was destiny that we went to the tropical Virgin Islands, even if we were only there a few days. There were five crucial things that happened on this super short, three-day "honeymoon." At first, I hated calling it that word, I preferred the title of this chapter:

1. *We bonded on the plane ride*

This was the first time we got to sit alone and really get to know each other. I opened up a bit about my upbringing and how I'd cared for my siblings because of my mom's drug benders. Doug was curious about my background but, again, he didn't pry. I could also tell he wasn't judging me.

Would his family judge me though? Doug's childhood was so cookie cutter that he admitted he had to convince his mom that he wouldn't take this marriage as a joke. His father, Doug Sr., and brother Matthew kept teasing that I would be a mail-order bride from Russia named "Olga." They still affectionately call me Olga.

We knocked out all the important topics, and realized we had the same values and so much in common, everything from politics (both middle of the road) to how many kids we wanted (two or three, plus adopt one or two).

That was a huge turning point for us. That and the fact that we had the same plan for life and a similar sense of humor. I read a study somewhere tooling around online recently that 58 percent of women say lack of sense of humor is a deal breaker; it came fourth on a list of the Top 5, after disheveled, lazy and needy. I'd concur with all of those. He made me laugh so much, I was beginning to feel relaxed and comfortable.

2. *We had a tiny bathroom*

One of the real-life situations we were immediately thrown into was sharing a bathroom. Our hotel room had a really small bathroom, like the size of an egg. So small both of us could barely fit in there at the same time. Nope, no intimate jacuzzi tub for these newlyweds. Sounds silly but almost every couple I know out there has had to negotiate toilet seats up or down, long hairs in the sink, toothpaste tubes squeezed from top or bottom and globs in the sink, tampon discards. It's all very intimate. And you have to be on the same page about the embarrassing stuff—like farting, which is not a turn-on for me in any way. Doug felt the same and had no desire for me to be one of those women who jumps up on a guy's lap and lets one rip. I don't give a hoot if you're one of those tooters—no judgment—but I'm just not. Neither of us wanted to pee with the door open, though as time went on, I relaxed that policy but Doug still doesn't want me to see him standing at the toilet. When it came to pooping, we both agreed on a closed-door policy, so as not to ruin intimacy. I couldn't even do it with the door closed. Our bathroom was so tiny and the door so thin, the ol' turn the shower on trick didn't work. So I'd go down to the lobby bathroom to do my business. We had no need to poop in front of each other and still don't to this day. Yes, I have no filter but don't you like it that way?

Anyway, the best thing I discovered about Doug's bathroom habits is that he likes to hum while getting ready. Aww, I know.

3. *We wore bathing suits*

Forget Viagra, skin is one of the most powerful aphrodisiacs. In St. Thomas Doug and I didn't have to try very hard to be hot and bothered. We frolicked on the beach, as Doug said so eloquently, "next to each other in our underwear."

4. *We kissed*

By the last night of our honeymoon, okay I'll call it that now, Doug and I had serious chemistry and we were inflamed with desire. Wait, that sounds like an STD. Seriously, there was so much buildup, we wanted each other *bad*. Our first kiss was about a week into our marriage. We were having dinner at Mafolie hotel. The view from their restaurant is absolutely breathtaking. Mafolie sits on top of a mountain and gives you a view of what seems to be all of St. Thomas. It was romantic and beautiful. We were both shy and bashful for our first kiss, but after that we couldn't stop kissing each other.

5. *I touched his ween*

I still wasn't near ready to do the deed. But we were thirsty, and I'm not talking about wanting more wine. As we all know by now, I can get a little awkward and Chatty Cathy in intimate moments. Instead of being sexy, I talk too much.

"Now that I'm your wife, don't you think I should see my husband's penis?"

"Yeah, of course!" Doug said gleefully.

Poor guy. I wasn't trying to be a tease—but I was such a tease.

I grabbed his penis and I was totally into it, 100 percent satisfied. But I'm so insecure in bed and incapable of letting my guard down so fast. We were hot and heavy, but I subconsciously dialed it down because I was uncomfortable. I made probably THE worst joke a woman can make about a man. Especially while she's holding his penis. For the first time.

"I thought maybe it'd be a little bigger."

Who says that?

I do, that's who.

Doug just had his manhood questioned. His balls busted. And you know what he did? He *laughed*. He got the *joke*. He got *me*. Quirks and all.

I'd just made a dig about his pee-pee and he didn't bat an eye. He was confident in his penis size and how to use it. This guy was impossible to offend. He was unflappable. For me, a woman who came from a background of total and utter flappableness at all times, his Zen attitude was calming. What I admired so much about Doug right off the bat was his ability to make everyone around him feel comfortable. I could tell he was in no rush with me and understood if our love was meant to be, then so be it. He wasn't pushing anything. He made me feel so safe.

Sidebar: Top 10 Tips For Honeymooners!

Okay, mine was really bizarre but I think I learned some valuable intel in St. Thomas that is universal:

1. Consider a mini-moon

Three days was plenty. We never had enough time to get sick of each other! If we couldn't stand the sight of each other after that little amount of time, it would have been a sign that we were doomed.

2. Play the Newlywed Game

Try asking your new spouse questions you don't know the answers to—I guarantee you will find out fascinating new information. Hopefully it doesn't cause a fight! Sorry in advance if it does. But you should probably know anyway.

3. Don't over-plan

I'm guessing your wedding was stressful. Remove one less thing on your list and just wing it when you get to your honeymoon destination. It makes it more exciting and less stressful than having to stick to a schedule.

4. *No pressure about sex*

If you go right after your wedding, you're going to be tired. Don't put insane expectations on your sex life during your honeymoon. You don't have to be porn stars and set a world record for fornication. If it makes you feel better, Doug and I didn't even have sex on our honeymoon.

5. *Create your own romance*

You don't need to spend a lot of money adorning your room with rose petals and expensive bottles of champagne. Sometimes a simple walk on the beach at sunset does the trick. Save money from spa trips and bring your own oils and lotions. Massage each other. If you really want to make it steamy, slather the lotion on each other while you're naked. This will definitely be more intimate and memorable (and more enjoyable!) than a trip to the spa! And, you'll save $.

6. *Befriend a local*

They might take you off the beaten path to the less touristy, more romantic spots. They will help point you in the right direction for sightseeing and shopping. And if you're in a foreign country they can help you understand proper payments for taxi, tips, etc. so you don't get scammed by the locals.

7. *Treat yourself to one fancy dinner*

Sure, it's fun to lay in bed together all day but getting dressed up to the nines and drinking wine over candlelight instigates flirting. Sometimes we forget to get dressed up for our partner. Take time to make sure you look incredible. This will make you feel good about you AND your spouse will feel good about it, too.

8. *Be flexible*

Do you and your spouse disagree about activities? Does one of you like to run around sightseeing all day and the other like to lie on the beach like slugs? Prepare yourself mentally for everything, come what may. It's a chillaxed philosophy that can help avoid fights.

9. *Unplug*

This is a no-brainer and extremely hard to do but worth it. Tune out the outside noise—no SnapChat, Twitter, Instagram, Facebook or emails—and focus all of your attention on your spouse. For Doug and me I add TV to this. He loves his TV on at all times of the day, but when on vacation/honeymoon the TV was unplugged. This ensures we spend *quality* time together. It also ensures we interact together more. Plus, who wants to watch something you can watch anywhere when you're on an exotic trip?!

10. *Let go of expectations*

You can honeymoon in a tree house or you can be on the most romantic island in the world. Either way I guarantee you will encounter a problem on your trip. (Don't hate me for calling out the obvious. I'm a realist.) Be prepared to run late, struggle finding a cab, get a little lost, etc. Don't let these minor inconveniences cause a fight between you two or allow you to be grumpy. When all is said and done, you're with the person you love and plan on spending the rest of your life with. At the end of the day, being together is the only thing that matters.

CHAPTER 5

Shacking Ups And Downs

What does a lesbian bring on her second date? A U-Haul!

This is a classic joke by comedian Lea Delaria, who plays Big Boo on the show *Orange Is the New Black*. Doug and I are obviously not lesbians, but maybe we could get an honorary patch or something after moving in together one week after meeting.

When we returned to New York, we were no longer separate individuals, just Jamie and Doug. For the first time, in our hearts, we'd officially become The Hehners.

Team Damie was now cohabitating, which was totally insane, considering it takes some couples (including lesbians, don't send me angry tweets for stereotyping, it's a joke!) a really long time to take the plunge. Google "moving in together" and a million articles pop up offering the important "signs" and "ways to know" when it's the right time. I kid you not, here are some of the indicators:

- *"You don't feel a sense of pressure"*

- *"You've talked about finances"*

- *"You really, really like each other"*

- *"Your lifestyles are compatible"*

- *"You've survived major disagreements"*

- *"You've traveled together" (check)*

- *"You've discussed your expectations"*

- *"You've defined your deal breakers"*

I could go on and on with this list. It's like having a baby. If you wait for the "right" time, you ain't never havin' yo baby!

All of these signs are great on paper but the reality is, even if you think you've got them covered, you have no friggin' idea what you're in for. I find the deal breakers one particularly amusing because you can't possibly know all the deal breakers before you get there. For example, if I'd dated Doug for five years I still might not have had a clue that he secretly loves to buy gifts and gadgets from those "As Seen On TV" commercials. Our drawers today are crammed with peelers that make swirls, jewelry cleaners, and special glasses that find golf balls in the dark.

But let me go back to when we first moved in together because I had more important things to worry about than Doug's minor shopping compulsion. I was making a home with the guy but didn't even feel comfortable walking around without a bra on. Shouldn't that be the most important sign you're ready? I don't see that in any article online! This would be my list:

- *Feel comfy walking around without a bra*

- *Have smelled each other's morning breath and are okay*

- *Agree on specific sexual experimentations, wink wink*

- *Confirm that your pet and partner are BFF*

- *Poop while partner is home.*

Even if you have to turn on the shower or spray after so they don't smell it. It's okay. Just make sure you don't have to hold it all night until he/she finally leaves for work in the morning! I think everybody has done that at least once or 10 times in their life.

JAMIE OTIS | Wifey 101

This was all so foreign. Neither of us had ever officially lived with a significant other. I lived at Stan's full-time for a total of about three or four months, and Doug had owned a house at one point but an ex had only stayed there on and off. That's it. So, this was the blind leading the blind.

Also, we were coming from very different places. I'd lived on my own since the age of 18 but I'd also lived with a bunch of random people starting in sixth grade. I lived with the neighbor Dean, then with my mom's best friend Patty, my mom's ex-boyfriend, Andy, and one of my childhood friends, Amber. Because I've been on my own and had even had three kids living with me at one point, I had a fully stocked apartment in NYC. Doug had just come from living with his parents and literally brought nothing with him other than his clothes. He didn't even have his own shampoo. I had no idea he was such a bachelor and it was eye-opening. When we moved into our first new home, he was so proud of himself for buying a set of dishes, even though I already had servings for six and had no intention of getting rid of mine. (We compromised and now have all the dishes stacked together in the cupboard.)

The stuff we were bringing with us also included our "baggage." My only other roommates had been my younger siblings and my foster child. Back when I got custody, I was the boss and it was my way or the highway. I delegated chores, left them to-do lists and would praise them after they completed a task. It had to be an entirely different dynamic with a husband, right? I certainly didn't want to be a nag or feel like his mother. Right off the bat I was tested when I'd have to drag Doug out of bed in the morning. It was literally that whole "Just 10 more minutes, Mom!" thing and it took every fiber in my body not to go in the henpecking/maternal direction. I wanted to scream, "Get up and get your butt in gear!" but I knew that was a one-way ticket to Divorce-ville. The other option was just being late everywhere we went. Neither of these choices are very fun. Honestly, Doug's trouble waking up—something we still haven't mastered—was a wake-up call that this wasn't going to be easy in any way.

We still had so much to learn about each other but had to find common ground and compromise on a host of different issues—the inane (decorating), the logistical (splitting the bills), and the emotional (SEX, dum DUM DUM scary music). We also were setting up the fundamental dynamic of our relationship. Doug and I were a team now but maintaining our individuality was important, too. We had to deal with the needs of "Damie," as well as Jamie's and Doug's. Sorry, I'm speaking in third person and will stop that STAT.

Here are a few things we weren't on the same page about at first but managed to find middle ground:

Decorating

THE PROBLEM: I didn't think I was picky about the style of our living space until Doug pointed out just how controlling

I could be. If controlling means I would pick something out, like a couch, sell him hard on it and just wait for him to nod his head yes, fine, guilty! Since Doug had almost nothing, I brought a lot of my stuff, so I admit maybe our decor leaned toward the girlie side.

THE COMPROMISE: Doug realized that the reason I needed to be surrounded by my things was related to my past. Everything I'd bought in my life was a reminder of how far I'd come. I was proud of what I'd accomplished on my own with no help and I liked to reflect back on that time. Once he figured that out, he was totally fine. Plus, a lot of the stuff I brought is very sentimental to me. For example, I still have decorations that my sisters made in art class for me. How could I possibly get rid of these?! My compromise was to happily include him in the decision-making, so he picked out our TVs and nightstands. Looking back now I wish I had trusted Doug more with his interior designing skills. The man is good! He can turn any room into a cozy, comfy space.

Food

THE PROBLEM: I was duped by Doug's family and friends when they claimed he loved to cook. And I just assumed he loved to eat healthy because, c'mon, look at his body. This was a huge misconception and a rude awakening. When he lived at home, Doug had all his meals cooked for him by his dad. When we moved in together, it became crystal clear that he was a true bachelor, who wasn't going to make me a delicious, healthy 10-course meal. He can actually cook very well but he just prefers not to. His meal of choice comes from the freezer aisle. When Doug went grocery shopping (this was a rare occurrence) we would have a freezer filled with lean cuisine, frozen lasagna, pasta, ice cream and ice pops. Doug's idea of fine dining was fried chicken nuggets on a bagel with cheese, ranch, and bbq sauce. (Insider note: This was the first meal he "cooked" for me.) Before I met him, I was a healthy eater but because I wanted us to jive and make my husband happy, I started eating like him. I mean, it wasn't hard. The food he makes is absolutely delicious. It's just terribly unhealthy. I'll be the first to admit I'm a terrible cook, so when we weren't eating Doug's favorite frozen, sodium-filled snacks, TV dinners or cereal, we ordered in. This sucks because I not only gained weight, we weren't eating together as a couple. He'd sit in front of the TV eating on a TV tray, while I stood at the counter because I hate sitting down (more on that in a second).

THE COMPROMISE: If we ordered in, he agreed to eat sushi sometimes, even though he doesn't like it much. More important, I made a concerted effort to learn how to cook because when we have kids, I need to know how to make them nutritious meals. And you know what? I've actually been enjoying this whole cooking thing. A friend of Doug's and mine told me about a food service called Blue Apron. They deliver you complete meals with recipes included right to your front door step. This has been a life saver for me and Doug. It's the easiest way to get new fruits and veggies

JAMIE OTIS | Wifey 101

in your diet. It also completely eliminates the age old problem of not having time to go to the grocery store so you just order out. I wasn't so good at making these meals at first, but my foodie friend Erica Eckman from *Everything Erica* inspired me to keep on practicing and I finally cooked a meal that Doug loved—meatballs, celeriac mash and kale. Okay, he hated the kale, but I'll take two out of three. That was enough to get a spot on my blog, JamieOtis.com, shameless plug over now. Now that I'm making meals I'm all sorts of proud of, Doug and I eat together as much as possible at our dining room table. No phone, no TV, and we have to look in each other's eyes, whether I've burnt dinner or not!

Sharing

THE PROBLEM: I want to be close to Doug 24/7, and that includes stealing his T-shirts, sweatpants and boxer shorts, and wearing them to bed. I think it is endearing and cute, but Doug couldn't disagree more. He absolutely despises when I do this; it eats him up inside. He'll say, "Jamie, don't wear that shirt," or "Jamie, that doesn't fit." And I'll say, "Yes, it does, Douglas," even when I've rolled the waistband of his sweatpants over like 20 times. You should see the look on his face when he's run out of underwear because of me. It's not pretty. As Doug has explained, as the oldest of three kids in his family, his brother and sister used to take all of his toys and clothes and ruin them, so it drives him crazy when I do it, too.

THE COMPROMISE: For our first Christmas, Doug got me my very own pack of men's boxer shorts, size small. Sadly, he didn't get it. I didn't want just any ol', new underpants, I wanted *his*. I like wearing his clothes because they smell like him and I feel closer to him. I realize this is weird, especially with underwear. (C'mon, guys, get your head out of the gutter. Obviously I only wear them when they're clean.) Truthfully, his underwear is just really comfy. I've yet to find a pair of PJs as comfy as my hubby's boxer briefs and T-shirt. The new ones he bought me just aren't the same. I'm not sure if my husband knows this, but I re-gifted the new boxers to my nephew. This issue has not been solved and I'm sorry my dear Douglas, but I fear this is a losing battle for you. Kisses.

Sex

THE PROBLEM: I did not have sex with Doug for the first eight weeks of our marriage—the entire experiment time and then some. Even though we lived together. I have a rule about not sleeping with guys until at least two months in and I wasn't about to throw that out the window just because we were sleeping under one roof or under one comforter. Plus, this is my way of making sure I am respected and truly loved before I give my goodies—or reveal my awkward sexual tendencies. I know it sounds a bit neurotic, but it's saved me from a lot of heartbreak and helped me filter out the guys who only wanted one thing. My Momma may have been a bit hit or miss while growing up but she was dead on when she said most men only want one thing. I'm guessing most women have sex with their future spouse before they get married and if they haven't, they'll do it within a day or two of their weddings. Even if I have nothing in common with 99 percent of new brides on the sex topic, I do think the question of the amount of sexual activity you're "supposed" to have when you move in together is universal. And can be an issue if not discussed.

THE COMPROMISE: I was so fortunate that Doug was so patient and respected me so much, he waited until I was ready without complaint. He was rewarded for this admirable behavior with lots of wild humping and even blowjobs. Before Doug, I'd never been comfortable giving a man oral sex because of the abuse I'd gone through. But Doug made me feel so comfortable, I was so into him, so it was a big deal for me. I will say that because I'm sort of a prude, Doug's dirty sense of humor was an adjustment for me. Not long after we moved in together, he showed me a video of him doing stand-up comedy. When it got to the part about his mom's favorite dildo being named after a Bruce Lee movie called *Enter the Dragon*, I'd seen enough. I can laugh about it now but I didn't really find it funny then! I just never find dirty jokes to be all that funny. Doug has toned it down a little, and I've loosened up a lot.

Punctuality

THE PROBLEM: Doug is *always* late. I think it's rude but he doesn't care. I try to explain to him that when we are late it makes it seem like we think our time is more valuable than those who we make wait for us. He just doesn't get it.

THE COMPROMISE: I will say, one of Doug's best qualities is that if something is bothering me, he will try to change and work on it. He does listen and that means the world to me. But in this case, I've tried yelling, I've tried having a calm conversation. Neither and nothing has worked. I've even tried lying about the start time of events but he picked up on that and was still late. He's also gotten very clever about his excuses, like blaming our dog Lady for being sick. Things that are hard to argue with. This is a work in progress, and I'll keep you posted. If anyone has any ideas, please tweet me.

Private Time

THE PROBLEM: Doug and I have fundamentally different ways to relax. After work, he needs to decompress, which means lying on the couch watching TV or going up to our bedroom to putter around by himself. I, on the other hand, do not crave down-time. As I mentioned, if I'm not moving, I'm not getting anything accomplished. We had one TV growing up and usually the news was on so I've never been one to gravitate toward the TV. That's not really my idea of a good time. It drives Doug crazy that I never get pop culture references to TV shows or movies, except for the phrase "Slippery little suckers" from *Pretty Woman*. On top of that, I hate being alone. I never had anyone nagging me growing up, so I love being around people. I have four siblings and they have always been a huge part of my life. I've always enjoyed them. After years and years of always having them by my side it's "lonely" for me to not have anyone around. If it was scientifically possible to be conjoined to Doug, like sewn together, I would do it.

THE COMPROMISE: I've learned to relax in front of the TV a tiny bit so I can have quality time with my husband. After not being able to mutually agree on *Scandal*, *Breaking Bad* and *Gossip Girl*, Doug and I finally discovered a mutual love for *Homeland*, *The Walking Dead* and *Making a Murderer*. I'm getting better about letting Doug have some alone-time right when he gets home from work, and he's gotten better about giving me a tiny bit of attention before he disappears so it doesn't feel like he's avoiding me. I've allowed him to claim our bedroom as his man cave and, drum roll please, he's now got his own bathroom. I think he deserved it because he needed to masturbate a lot when I wasn't ready for sex. At first, he wouldn't even let me pee in his bathroom and made me go out to my bathroom in the hallway in the middle of the night. He's gotten over that.

Chores

THE PROBLEM: Because I'd made a conscious effort not to be a nag, we never made an official list of who does what. At first, we equally picked up after each other, and Doug would wash his dishes and fold his clothes perfectly and put them away. But as time went on, and we got more comfy around each other, that blew up. Doug's nightstand is currently stacked with half-drunk Gatorade bottles and dirty dishes, often with fluffernutter or gum stuck to them. Doug is also a bit of a hoarder—he doesn't throw anything away, and has just as many clothes and shoes as I do. He even has his lifeguard shirts and sweatpants from college that are riddled with holes but refuses to get rid of them. He even refuses to throw away holey underwear. I grew up with constant clutter and filth, so it drives me crazy.

THE COMPROMISE: At first I cleaned Doug's nightstand but I didn't want to turn into a maid. So now I don't and that means those dishes can stay there as long as a week sometimes. It's his side to deal with. Not worth us fighting over it. I don't want to touch his bathroom. At one point there was black mold and mildew on the bottom of his shower floor but I just left it. It's his bathroom. Doug's adamant that no guests use his bathroom because he thinks sharing it with strangers is "dirty." If he wanted me to help keep it tidy he'd let me know. I don't think it bothers him one bit. And since our guests and I don't shower in there I shouldn't let it bother me either. That's how the "nagging mommy" role stays out of the picture. And what about the holey undies? Yeah, sorry hubs, but I have to admit I toss those out the moment I come across them in the laundry basket. I'll buy you underwear that is fully intact!

So there you go. Those were our biggest issues when we shacked up, warts and all. I think at the very beginning we tried to be too perfect, almost competitive with each other for "Spouse of the Year." But keeping up that façade was exhausting and it backfired. It ended up biting us both in the butt.

A couple weeks after Doug and I moved in together, I almost divorced him because he lied to me about smoking a cigarette. Everyone thought I'd made a mountain out of a molehill but hear me out.

Doug and I had fallen madly, deeply in puppy love after living together for about two weeks and dry-humping our faces off. I was ready to bring Doug upstate to see where I grew up. This HAD to happen before the end of the experiment because it was imperative that he and my family get along. I'd never taken a man home to meet my family, let alone see the trailer park where so many horrible things had happened to my siblings and me. But I knew now that I trusted Doug and wanted to open up to him about my mom's addictions and maybe even more. I felt like he needed to know this info and that he could handle it. I wanted to make sure he fit in with my family and that my family was comfortable with him. If that didn't happen, game over.

When we got up there, I was anxious and overwhelmed but Doug was his usual wonderful and supportive self, even when he saw the trailer park lined with tin homes a quarter of the size of his and was later badgered by my older sister Joh. My sister just wanted to protect me, but of course that just embarrassed me. She kept lecturing the crap out of him about being a good husband, and I wanted to scream, "Shut up!" She told him how hard married life is and that he is in for a rude awakening if he thinks it's rainbows and sunshine. But I didn't want to make things more stressful so I bit my lip. Besides, Doug seemed to take it in stride 100 percent. (P.S. she was definitely right, too!) He may have been a suburban boy but he sure had fun with my siblings and their significant others, four-wheeling and mud-bogging like a good ol' redneck.

My nieces and nephews swarmed all over Doug and he loved every minute of it. He ran around outside chasing after them and got out the football and played catch.

While we were at my old trailer park, Doug and I went for a walk out back. There was a nice little river that ran right behind the park and I always went there to clear my mind and think. It was the only place to hide from all the windows with eyes peeping out and thin walls with ears listening that surrounded me at every angle in the trailer park. It was here that I opened up for the first time and gave Doug a deeper understanding of what my life had been like up until now. I explained how my stepdad would come over to the trailer drunk as a skunk demanding to see his daughter, banging his fists up and down the front door. Leah and I would hide in her bedroom with the lights off hoping and praying he'd just go away. We thought if we were quiet enough he'd think we weren't there. I shared some of my deepest, darkest secrets but I didn't share them all. I wasn't ready. Doug handled what I did reveal like a champ. He seemed to just get it. He wasn't judgmental or ashamed to be with me. It made me feel good and like I could talk to him about anything. But I couldn't tell him those other secrets I was hiding. Not yet. It was too much all at once.

When we left, my heart was full and happy. The trip couldn't have gone any better. I knew I was in that puppy love before but now I was infatuated, absolutely head over heels for Doug. In the car ride home, we talked about where we should raise our kids, in the country or in the suburbs? We agreed that we wanted a backyard so he could mow it and I could plant a garden. We were so on the same page and I'd never felt more secure.

It seemed too good to be true.

When we got back to New York City, Doug dropped me off at the front door, told me to take the luggage and Lady inside, and he would park the car at our garage down the street. I took Lady for a walk and when I got back 25 minutes later, Doug still wasn't back. I called and texted him but there was no answer. I was starting to get worried when he finally walked through the door.

I went to kiss him and he tasted like a cigarette.

"Have you been smoking?" I asked. I was dumbfounded for a second, then remembered that on our honeymoon, I spotted a pack of cigarettes in his bag but I really thought nothing of it. He said some excuse like, "Oh, I was just gonna give those to the hotel workers." Something so strange like that, and you know when you're smitten, you're kind of dumb? I was that dumb girl and I said, "Oh, yeah, whatever!" Another time, I saw a half a pack in his car. I said, "What are *these* doing in here?" I had no idea he smoked. And he goes "Oh, yeah, those are so old, I don't know." And he threw them out the window. Just like that. He rolled down the window and tossed them out to the sidewalk. So strange. Still, I was so gaga over him and not catching on. I literally had no idea he ever smoked. That's the thing, I filled out the paperwork, and I was really honest and precise about what I wanted. One of the questions was "Are you a smoker? Do you want to be with a smoker?" And I was like, "NO. NO." And he knew that.

Back to the unfolding drama…I asked Doug, "Have you been smoking?"

"What? No!" Doug said defensively.

"You taste like an ashtray."

"I walked though a group of people smoking."

It was 10 p.m. on a Sunday night. There was no crowd of people. Secondhand smoke doesn't just cling to a non-smoker's lips. Was I going crazy? He stunk like smoke.

"Douglas, why are you lying to me? Just admit you had a cigarette."

If Doug had told me, "You know what? This weekend was super-stressful for me and I needed a cigarette," I guarantee I would have said jokingly, "Oh my gosh I know, give me one, too!"

But Doug didn't say that. This is what he said:

"I swear on my mother's life."

I couldn't believe my ears. It was just one lie after another, so easily coming out of his filthy mouth. I had flashbacks to my childhood, all of those men who lied through nicotine-stained teeth about where they'd been and whom they'd been with. I knew a liar when I heard one. I was an expert. Didn't Doug know that by now?

He obviously thought I was stupid and continued to swear up and down on his mother's life. What an immature, insensitive brat, I thought, fuming. Doug's lies were like a punch in the gut. If he had just explained to me that he was trying to quit and had relapses sometimes I wouldn't have cared nearly as much. All of this wouldn't have ever happened. I was so hurt and so disappointed and felt so foolish—all the walls I'd worked so hard to tear down went right back up. Steel-enforced this time. I was Fort Knox.

Doug could feel the barrier going up and the more I ignored him, the more he demanded my attention. But I couldn't even look at him, I was so disgusted. I got in my jammies and fell into bed.

This is the part that nobody knows.

Suddenly, Doug crawled over to me and got right in my face.

"Jamie, I promise you..." he began, tears rolling down this face.

I snapped. Bad men had done this to me all my life. I had visions of being locked in the bathroom and a prisoner in my own car while they demanded that I listen to them, tears rolling down their face. Uh-uh. No way, buddy. Not this time.

"DO NOT EVER GET THAT CLOSE TO ME AGAIN," I said loudly and forcefully. "GET OFF OF ME AND LEAVE ME ALONE."

Doug moved away from me immediately. I think he got scared of me.

"You're right," he broke down. "I had a cigarette."

Of course he did, but this was the least important revelation. I'd only known my new husband for a few weeks and now, seemingly out of the blue, I was uncertain if I was safe or could trust him.

Was this the real him?

I had no way of knowing. No fancy wedding, tropical honeymoon, or puppy love could remove the fact that I really knew nothing about him. He was still very much a stranger.

What I did know was that I was DONE with Doug Hehner.

CHAPTER 6

The Truth Hurts (And Sets You Free)

Do nothing secretly; for Time sees and hears all things. And discloses all —Sophocles

Quoting an ancient Greek philosopher is pretty pretentious, I know, but I'm just trying to prove an important point here and didn't want to use someone like a Kardashian: We've all been keeping secrets since the beginning of time, for various reasons, and 90 percent of the time end up getting caught. This does not excuse Doug for lying. Turns out he was more of a smoker than he let on, thought he could quit but was having trouble going cold turkey. Knowing I was adamantly against smoking, he didn't want to lose me so he hid it. Fine. I get that. What I couldn't deal with were the abhorrent lies he told after I caught him. Plus, I'd made it clear that drugs, alcohol, and cigarettes were deal breakers. Strike one. I threw in that baseball reference for Douglas.

The night after the "Great Smokeout of 2014," Doug and I had a date scheduled. Of course, you think date night equals lovey-dovey but we were not "the happy couple" anymore. There was no way I could phone it in. I wasn't feeling it and refused to force it. Everybody gave me a little attitude, like I was an overreacting, unforgiving snot and should just accept Doug's apology because he cried. I wanted to scream, "What are you, nuts? Every guy cries and comes back 10 times worse!" I'd seen this all before with my older sister's, mom's and my exes. Doug was upset that I kept lumping him in with every man who'd ever hurt my family or me. But at this point he hasn't proven himself to be any different than the rest of them.

We only had a couple weeks left in the trial period of the experiment and I was close to breaking up with him. We'd promised each other we'd give this marriage at least six months but I was having serious doubts I'd make it that long. I also promised I'd give it 100 percent so I agreed to go see a psychologist for couple's counseling one last time before our six-week experiment ended.

Everyone else had made me feel like I was exaggerating—the psychologist was different. He was the first person to say to me, "It's okay for you to feel how you're feeling, given your past." Finally someone understood me. But he didn't let me off the hook.

"Make a mental note, Jamie, but don't call it quits after you've come this far," he added. He was right. If Doug and I were just dating it definitely would be over. That was my routine while dating. But that's exactly why I did this experiment. So I wouldn't just throw in the towel at the first sign of trouble. Before, it was one red flag and I was out. There was so much good about my marriage that I'd just tossed aside when Doug lied about the cigarette.

"I genuinely believe Doug is very, very sorry," the psychologist explained. "Don't forget what happened, but don't focus on it. Move forward. If it happens again, then you know this is a big problem." The psychologist gave me the guidance I'd been craving and I ate it up. He saved our marriage (for the first time), and he saved me as a wife and a partner.

Doug and I left the psychologist's office holding hands, though my guard was still up. So far, my husband had proven to be loving, patient and respectful, so why was I having so many issues trusting him? What other dirty secrets did Doug have that I didn't know about?

I knew there had to be more than just smoking. I knew from experience—because I had several big secrets I'd been withholding, too. Sure, you can call me a hypocrite now. I deserve that.

I'd already opened up to Doug about my upbringing and my mom's addictions but that was easy compared to what else I needed to tell him. It was so scary. On the one hand, Doug had never been one to judge or pry. On the other hand, he was a happy-go-lucky kind of guy, who shied away from talking about anything too heavy. It made him uncomfortable, I'd noticed, and he didn't know how to react.

In a solid marriage, are you required to tell your husband absolutely *everything*? How much does your spouse need to know? It seems like the answer is obvious—of course your life partner needs to know *everything*! But it's not that simple. Doug and I barely knew each other and we were on this fast track, so when was it appropriate to tell him I'd been molested repeatedly for four years of my childhood? We hadn't even had sex yet. He might have understood why I was making him wait so long if I'd been able to explain that when I have sex I feel manipulated and used. This is always the question in my mind: "Is sex only for his pleasure or does he truly love me? Is he just trying to get in my pants for a good time?"

I knew it was crucial for me to tell Doug and yet I couldn't bring myself to do it, even though it was something that was affecting us drastically in the bedroom. Doug said from day one that a good sex life is very important to him. I agree. I knew that I wasn't helping our relationship grow by being Ms. Prude, but I didn't know how to be Mrs. Back-scratching Sex Kitten. Logically I know what happened when I was a kid wasn't my fault, but I was so ashamed of what had happened. I really didn't know what Doug would think. The idea of sitting down and trying to nonchalantly bring up this topic made me nauseous. Like how would I even try? What was the best way to introduce the topic? I knew it would make him uncomfortable, which then would make me uncomfortable. I just didn't know how to go about it. And I knew if I could just get it out there that it'd solve a lot of his insecurity thinking I'm just not attracted to him and that was part of the reason we struggled sexually so much.

The other huge secret I was hiding was also from my past but could have a huge effect on our future. I can't believe I am admitting this, but I actually had two abortions—not just one—from two different men. There is *nothing* I am more ashamed of in my life than this. I don't even know how to write about this, let alone talk about it. But I'm going to try.

Nothing made me feel more "trailer trash," like all the kids said I was, than this. I'm hoping the truth really does set you free because the guilt and shame of this has been weighing me down for years. The first time, as I explained earlier, was with Ted. I was eighteen, going to college and working at a restaurant when I found out. I called my boss and told him I needed two days off.

"What, are you getting an abortion or something?" I hung up on him, so distraught and humiliated and feeling like the biggest loser. How did he know? I'll never forget that he said that to me so callously. Ted was just as callous. He was so jealous and possessive of me but couldn't care less about our baby. "I don't care if you have it or don't," he told me. Ted showed up for the procedure but was so unruly he was escorted out of the building. Afterward, I was in the temporary hospital bed hyperventilating and puking into a paper bag. Then Ted disappeared the next day to go get drunk and high with his friends.

When I found out I was pregnant again I was in nursing school, had custody of my sisters and was still dating Burt, the boyfriend who got drunk and took his shotgun out when someone insulted his sister. When I found out I was pregnant again, I started bawling. I was shocked when it happened the first time but how could this have happened *again*? It was definitely my fault. The women in my family are fertile Myrtles. I knew this. Both times I'd been on birth control but wasn't taking it properly. I'd skip a day or take two in one day, thinking I'd "catch up." I was older this time and I should have learned from the first time. Why didn't I take my birth control pills exactly like they were prescribed? Everyone knows the "pull-out" method doesn't always work. Why wasn't I more careful? How did I find myself here, *again*?

The first person I told was Burt. He was three years younger than me so you can imagine his reaction. Nothing but fear. His reaction was typical of his age. He wasn't ready to be a dad. He hadn't planned on being a dad at all. We were both in college and neither of us had good jobs. But he told me no matter what I decided he'd support my decision. I genuinely appreciated him letting me decide but I really wish I could have had some sort of advice or guidance. I yearned for someone to tell me what the right thing for this pregnancy and me was.

I called my friend Elya, who was living in Germany because her husband was in the Army and stationed there. The first time I confided in Elya and my other best friend, who went to a party and told everyone I was pregnant. That ruined our ten-year friendship overnight. This time, Elya was the only person I told. The first thing she said was that I should just have the baby because it's a sin to have an abortion. I knew she was right, but I called her every day and talked to her for hours about what both options looked like. Elya stood firm on not having an abortion because it wasn't fair to the helpless baby. I cried about already struggling just taking care of my sisters. I scraped pennies just to keep the heat on and make sure dinner was on the table for them every night. How could I add a baby into this? Not to mention, I just caught Burt smoking dope with the sixteen-year-old neighbor boy. How could I trust that he'd straighten up in time to be a dad? The only thing I knew for certain was that I was not willing to bring a child into the world if it had to grow up the way I grew up.

I was anxious and miserable about doing the right thing. I knew Elya was right, it was a sin to have an abortion. Thank God she never threw it in my face that I'd already had one and two would make me the scum of the earth. Despite her insistence, something in me knew I wasn't able to be a good mom yet. Or was that just me being unsure of myself—or worse, selfish? I read articles online about abortions. Some claimed that the fetus isn't a "baby" until it is born. I didn't agree with that at all. I learned in nursing school that a heartbeat was first detectable at six to seven weeks and its little arms and legs developed soon after. How could I abort that? That *is* a baby. I read other articles that said every single egg and every single sperm could eventually be babies. If you looked at it that way, you'd be aborting the chance to have a baby with every single menstrual cycle. Well, that was just crazy talk too. I took the knowledge I gained from everything I researched and came to my own conclusion: If I had the abortion while the sperm and egg were still just a "mass of cells," then it would almost be the same as if the sperm never fertilized the egg. You may not agree with me (I don't blame ya) but that made me feel okay about doing what I thought was the only responsible option I had.

Aside from having a young, immature boyfriend who may or may not be there for this kid, I was in no way ready to be a parent, and I refused to be anything less than a loving, caring, devoted mom. I was still in college and had zero support system. My mom only came around when she felt like it or needed money. My grandparents completely turned their backs on my siblings and me. It seemed like the minute my mom became a full-blown drug addict my extended family wanted nothing to do with her or her kids. Not that they called to check in on us much before, either. I'm sure they just assumed we would turn out just like her. When my mom was evicted from the trailer you'd think maybe they'd call to see how us kids were holding up alone, fending for ourselves. Not once.

Who would help me take care of this baby? Could I do it all alone? I'd have a full list of responsibilities: Care for a newborn, go to school, work, take care of my siblings, make sure there was food, heat, and electricity. There was just no way. It wasn't an easy decision for me to have an abortion. I cried and cried and kept going back and forth, but I decided I better just do it before it was too late and that "mass of cells" developed a heartbeat and turned into a baby. I'd never felt so depressed, trapped, and alone. Lying in bed, my pillow soaked with tears, I prayed to God and looked down to my stomach, begging both for their forgiveness.

On the day of the procedure, I woke up drenched in panic sweat. No one aside from Burt and Elya knew I was pregnant. My boyfriend had left the day before to go on a trip with his cousin. As I walked into the clinic, my face was wet with tears and red with shame. But this time I didn't get sick after. I was just numb.

By the time I got home I was hunched over with excruciating abdominal pains and cramping, blood oozing out of me, tears streaming down my face. I buried my head into my pillow and sobbed loudly. I couldn't stop asking myself, "Why, why, why? Why did I let this happen again? Why didn't I just listen to Elya and keep the baby? I could've figured it out. I always figured it out. I was doing okay raising my siblings, this could have worked, too!" I was so despondent, I never wanted to have to leave my bedroom again.

I'm aware that putting this out there is going to upset a lot of people. First of all, I've kept these secrets for years. My mother doesn't know, my sisters have no idea, and, as I write this, I still have to tell my husband. This is my deepest, darkest secret that I've kept hidden for years. The shame associated with this is indescribable. I'd never in a million years encourage anyone to get an abortion but I also understand if it is something you feel is right for you.

A couple years after my second abortion, my baby sister Leah became unexpectedly pregnant. She was nineteen years old and unwed, living with her boyfriend's family. My older sister was eighteen and unwed when she first got pregnant. My mom was eighteen and unwed when she first got pregnant. Notice a trend here? Like my mom and older sister before her, not once did Leah think about having an abortion. We may be "redneck country folk" but we don't have abortions in my family. It's completely frowned upon. "If you play, you pay" is the motto. It's a responsibility you just deal with, whether or not it's right for you or the baby.

Now, when I look at my baby sister, I think about how much braver she is than I was and if I think about it for too long I just lose it. My mom and my older sister too. While I watch my nieces and nephews grow up I can't help but wonder, "What would I have been like as a mommy? Would I have had a boy or a girl? How old would they be now?" If my older sister and *baby* sister is doing an incredible job and made it work maybe I could have, too? What have I done?!

I live with embarrassment and disgust knowing I've had two abortions. Anyone who has ever had one must know how I feel. I'm not saying I made the wrong choice, but it wasn't an easy choice and isn't a decision I can easily live with either.

All I can say is that I never took these abortions lightly. I don't know if I'll ever be able to rid myself of the shame and guilt that planted roots in my soul after these abortions. Both times I found myself pregnant I was shocked. I was dazed and heartbroken, and I only did it because I was scared shitless of the aftermath. I had to make the best decision not only for me, but for the future of these babies as well. I was in no financial position, either time, to take care of them. I was already in over my head raising my siblings. Would it have been fair to my siblings if I had a child? Would I have been able to devote my time and attention to my sisters if I had a baby? More important, I was not willing to subject these babies to the kind of upbringing I had, in abject poverty with either an absent or abusive father. Neither Ted nor Burt would provide a happy home. I mean, Ted has been in jail at least once that I know of for sure since.

For those who are furious that I wouldn't even consider carrying the baby to term and put it up for adoption, I get it. Now that I'm older, I wish I had thought of this option more then. But let me tell you a little story (I've been a hypocrite a lot in life, but this is by far the worst):

My mom found out she was pregnant with me right before the new year. Mom's dad, Grandpa Chuck, frowned upon women having children out of wedlock, even more so if they weren't in a committed relationship. One night soon after, he walked into Mom's trailer to deliver groceries when she was having one of her wild card parties. There were black men in the living room, because my mom has always welcomed everyone into her home. Apparently, Grandpa Chuck stormed out. He was not happy.

"You don't know if that child will be born black or white," he railed at her later. Mom told me he demanded that she have an abortion. He didn't want a black grandchild. With no money, no partner, and no family support, Mom thought an abortion was the only way out. She couldn't handle the shame that came attached with a child who was conceived from a drunken, drug-induced, one-night stand.

This was the '80s, so when Mom went to the abortion clinic, she said she was forced to watch a video first. What came next scared the daylights out of her. It was a viewing of the actual abortion, the vacuum, large white hose, all of it. As they were aborting the woman's baby, she said she could see little pieces of baby coming out of her, the arms and the legs. Mom burst into tears and walked right out of the clinic. So yes, I thank God she didn't follow through. Otherwise, I wouldn't be here today. But there's a second part to the story:

After Mom decided not to abort me, she immediately began searching for adoption agencies. She went to the Yellow Pages of the phone book but couldn't find one in our rural area. She bought a newspaper and browsed ads in the personals section. She found a couple good candidates and called them, but didn't think any of them were the right fit. Finally, she inquired at social services, which gave her contact info for a reputable adoption agency. She procrastinated. Before she called them she wanted to be certain it was what she wanted. After thinking long and hard about all the pros and cons of adopting me out versus keeping me she decided it was the right decision to give me to a loving family that could provide everything I would need and want in life. The cons of keeping me far outweighed the pros of keeping me. It was the fear of neglecting me that made her scared to keep me when she was pregnant. And secretly, she didn't want to face the fact that she would have two children with different, unknown fathers. She felt an immense amount of shame in that.

A few days later, Mom placed the call. Once she stated her case with the adoption agency there was no turning back. Within a month, a lucky couple was chosen, a young couple from Long Island. He was a professor and she was a schoolteacher. They were so excited about adopting me. They'd been waiting a long time to have a child of their own. The young woman explained to my mom they already had a nursery set up and she was prepared to take time off work as soon as the baby came. The couple called often during the rest of mom's pregnancy, offering money to pay all of her expenses, including medical bills. My mom said she refused to take any of the money. She said it felt wrong, like they were buying her child.

I was born on June 15 at Cortland Memorial Hospital. Everything happened so quickly, the doctor walked in just as my head popped out. My mom's told me the story of how I was conceived and my delivery several times. She said when the doctor held me upside down by my ankles, I turned my head and we made eye contact. She said she knew babies can't see far, but she swore there was an instant connection between us.

"I took one look at you," she says, "and knew I couldn't go through with the adoption. You were just so beautiful."

The nurse let my mom hold me, as she explained that the Long Island couple was there and very excited for their new baby. My mom began crying.

"I can't let my baby go yet!" she wailed.

The nurse became annoyed with my mom. "This young couple came all this way," she chastised. "You promised them and they've already prepared their home for this baby." The nurse handed Mom the final papers to relinquish her rights to me. Then she reached for me, to bring to the couple. Mom wouldn't let go.

"I just can't."

She never signed the papers and the Long Island couple never got their baby. Mom decided to name me Jamie Nicole Otis. "Jamie" after her favorite character on the TV show *The Bionic Woman*, "Otis," after her first husband. She wanted me to have the same last name as herself and Johanna. He wasn't my father. That she was sure of but he was one of the four men who'd later take a paternity test.

My mom told me these stories because she wanted me to know that she went through great lengths to keep me. This story might seem heartwarming at first, but the more you think about it, you realize how twisted it is. Sometimes I wonder why on earth my mom felt that it was necessary to thoroughly explain how I was completely unwanted by her and our family and the extreme measures she went through to get rid of me, only to end up keeping me at the end. I know she meant well, but, to this day, it still causes pain and the feeling of being unwanted deep in my soul.

When they talk about "family cycles" it's so true: My grandma dropped out of high school and had my mom young, my mom dropped out of high school and got pregnant at 18 years old, and my older sister dropped out of high school and got pregnant at 18 years old. I was 18 years old (just graduated) when I got pregnant for the first time.

I didn't want to follow my mom's and grandma's path. I had just figured out how to go to college. I wanted to be somebody. Make something out of my life. I wanted to break the cycle. And most importantly, I wanted to be the best mom possible. I wanted to make sure my kids grew up without ever having to go to bed hungry, move a zillion times because of eviction notices, and the absolute last thing I wanted was for me to bring a child into this world who had to grow up without a daddy or a daddy and mommy who fought constantly.

The bottom line is that I'm pro-choice for a very personal reason. I believe every woman should have the right to choose. But I would never encourage or discourage anyone. However, I do *strongly* encourage all women who decide to have an abortion to not delay. By six to seven weeks, all major organs are beginning to form from the mass of cells growing in your body. Once those cells form into a heartbeat, hands and feet, it's impossible to say that it isn't a baby who would grow up to be a child one day.

I also stand with Planned Parenthood, which gave me free birth control and condoms when I was too poor to afford them myself. PP also covered the cost of my abortions when I was struggling to make ends meet and raising my siblings.

But I need to add this: Ladies, it is so important to take your birth control the way it's prescribed. If you're too immature or irresponsible, like I was, to follow the directions exactly, then go get an IUD or the arm implant. (After my second abortion I got an IUD immediately. Both the IUD and the arm implant are practically foolproof. This is an almost certain way to prevent an accidental pregnancy.) Learn from my mistakes. Abortion should not be used as a form of birth control.

Having said all of this, I don't know whether to hide in a dark, cold hole or reach out to every single woman who has ever had an abortion. One thing I've learned from having my life shared on TV is that we aren't alone in our problems. As of right now, I don't know anyone else who I could confide in who had an abortion because I refused to talk about it. I lived in denial and just suppressed my feelings. My goal is that by sharing this I will help at least one person know that they're not alone in this and hopefully we will be able to connect and support each other. Whether or not we made the right decision we have to live with it every day. There's a whole world out there viciously judging us for our choices. I hope that we can join together to support each other and shield each other from hurtful words and attacks. Lastly, I hope by being honest about my circumstances, what made me choose abortion(s), how it felt and what it *still feels like* will offer guidance to someone who may be in the most difficult situation, wondering whether or not to have an abortion. Research what is right for you!

I've learned that I can't change the past, I can only move forward. I'm one who believes in karma. What goes around comes around. It's no secret I can't wait to have babies. The most important goal I've ever had is to be a loving, caring mom. I want at least two or three kids and to adopt at least one or two on top of that. But my biggest fear is that I won't be able to have children. Every time you have an abortion it increases your risk of not being able to have babies. Do I even deserve to have kids after what I've done? Honestly, I don't know.

What I do know is that Doug needed to know about my abortions. If I could take anything away from my past it'd be this. I can deal with the rest but *me* having done this just kills me.

It would be so much easier not to talk about it and just push it way, way, way down. I've gotten by this far, but I am one who believes that you should be able to tell your partner everything. They deserve to know it all. And it will bring you closer together. Well, I should practice what I preach. As I'm typing this, I have not yet told him about having these abortions. I will before this book comes out though. I don't know when I'll bring it up. It will just have to come out naturally.

That's how I learned another of Doug's secrets that I'm not sure if he ever planned on telling me. Months into our marriage, I was working on making him a romantic YouTube video on my computer (no, not porn!) when I heard a scream.

"Doug?"

No answer.

"Doug?"

I ran into the other room and found Doug hunched over in pain. He'd opened a box and cut his knee on a staple. It was bleeding pretty badly. I cleaned and bandaged it, but I knew he needed stitches. In case we had a long wait in the ER, I offered Doug a Vicodin I had left over after a tooth surgery.

"No, no, no, no!" Doug said adamantly.

I was taken aback by his insistence.

"Why won't you take this?" I asked. He was pale as a ghost and grimacing in pain. I'd never seen him hurt so bad.

Doug revealed that he'd had a serious dependency on prescription pills after his shoulder surgery.

I was shocked.

Doug reluctantly told me the whole story. He'd been a star third baseman, so good in fact that he was inducted into his high school's Hall of Fame. He earned a scholarship to Pace University and after being named an "All-American" freshman year, was scouted by several Major League teams, including the Mets and the White Sox. But his junior year, when he was eligible to turn pro, he had two shoulder surgeries that ended his career. All Doug ever wanted was to be a professional baseball player. So many little boys want to play in the MLB but Doug actually had the talent to make it. He was on his way when his dream was shattered abruptly and permanently. He had no Plan B.

Baseball was Doug's life. Lost and aimless, he sank into a depression and became addicted to the pain pills prescribed after his injury. Doug had always been the captain of his teams, a leader and the life of the party. For two years, he was an incoherent zombie, suffering alone in the darkest period of his life. He lost weight and alienated his friends. He borrowed money from his parents to feed his habit. Nothing mattered to Doug. The pills took over his life and destroyed it.

This is Doug's story to tell so I'm going to let him tell it in his own words. Take it away, hubby:

> *Thanks, Jamie. I was a very popular kid and always a good student. I graduated in the top 20 percent of my class, was elected vice president of the Student Council and homecoming king. I started high school as a three-sport athlete—baseball, basketball and soccer—but baseball was my passion and my true talent. It wasn't a far-fetched dream to play in the majors, it was a reality. I*

felt like I could play with anybody and had the confidence I could do it.

Flash forward to 2002, my junior year in college. I was coming off a great summer league season and in touch with several professional sports teams. That's when I had my first surgery on my shoulder. It was a devastating injury; I remember crying after I heard the news. I had to red-shirt that year, which meant that I had to miss the entire baseball season. It took a year before I felt back to the same player as I was before my injury.

When I got back on the field, I had an okay season, but I had fewer professional scouts coming to the games, and not a lot of tryouts being offered. But not long after, my shoulder had that same dull stinging feeling, and after another MRI, it was revealed that I had another tear in my shoulder, and would need another surgery. It was a career-ending injury. As much as I tried to stay positive, it was a difficult pill to swallow (pun intended). Baseball was my life, my full-time job, my motivation, my home away from home. I was the captain of the team, the leader, and in a blink of an eye...gone.

I was introduced to pain medication before my first surgery in 2003, but I never heard of anyone using it to get high. The first few times I took Vicodin, I threw up. Thinking back, I remember the euphoria type feeling.

Everything was great, drinking was a lot more fun, and it never dawned on me that it was addicting.

I remember going through my first surgery, and having a consistent supply of pain killers. At the end, I started to feel that itch, and some withdrawal symptoms, which only lasted for a day or two, and I was back to normal. I had baseball to get back to, and it was never really an issue for me.

After my second surgery, it was a slippery slope. I got to the point where I started taking four, five, six at a time, and I felt like I needed them to sleep.

Eventually I found myself in a battle I'd never win. I struggled on and off with pain killer addiction. What started out as getting high off of a few Vicodin or Percocet, ended up building to a tolerance of taking six to seven Roxicets in a day. To put that in perspective, when I took Percocet it'd be three 5 mg pills, more than enough to keep me high. By the end, at my lowest point, I was taking seven 30 mg Roxicets.

It got to the point where my day was consumed with finding pills. I would drive all over New Jersey, it didn't matter where or how long the drive was. I couldn't function normally without them. That was my only focus when I woke up, and all I would be able to think about. I would cancel plans, I would avoid my family, I was a miserable person, until I found pills.

I'd borrow money from my parents and say it was for a bill I had to pay. I still feel embarrassed and ashamed about that. My rock bottom was stealing pills from my grandpa. I would go to see him, knowing that I would be able to grab a few pills, or that he would be sleeping, and I would be able to grab some without him knowing.

It got to the point for me that I was not taking pills to get high anymore, I was taking pills to stop the withdrawals. It's a feeling of constant discomfort, and restlessness, yawning constantly, and getting goose bumps when the wind blows on you or when someone touches you. I remember rolling over, back and forth constantly at night, feeling uneasy, and hot and sweating, but then feeling cold and sweaty. It is a feeling that I would not wish on anyone.

My friends were the first to intervene. I never did anything around my family or closest friends, nor did I ever tell them that I was using pills. I was always very secret about it. One day, I got a call from my parents asking me to come meet them for dinner. My friends had gone into my room earlier that day, and took the pills that I had in my nightstand, and gave them to my parents. My mom, dad, sister, and brother confronted me and that was the first time I ever admitted that I had a problem. I could not control myself.

I was able to quit cold turkey and got off pills for a while but then relapsed. I ended up going to local meetings two or three days a week for a while. I slowly started to get back into a normal routine, working on myself, and got a full-time job. I have the greatest group of friends, and the most loving family, because I put them through a lot, and they stuck by me the whole way. They never made me feel like a degenerate, or a piece of shit, even though I felt like one. I will never be able to take back the hurt, concern, and frustration that I put them through, and I will always feel in debt to them.

I do not think I would be here today if it wasn't for them. You can go to all of the meetings in the world, and educate yourself, and get a sponsor, but you will never quit unless you want to quit. It has to be your decision, and one that you have to make on your own, that is the only way that you will truly quit. At the end, I was able to mentally want to quit, and never look back. There have been a lot of people that I knew from high school, past jobs, acquaintances, who have overdosed and died over the last fifteen years. I'm sure they didn't want to die, but you lose sight of limits, and you never know when it is *too much. Unfortunately, that consequence is dying. I am lucky to be here.*

While Doug's progression in life had stopped, all of his friends were just graduating college and getting married and having children. It was a major wakeup call. Luckily, Doug had a great support system, and with the help of his friends and family, he made a conscious decision to kick his addiction. He's been drug-free for nearly a decade now.

Doug bravely opened up so outwardly. I embraced him with open arms and love. Inside, though, I was freaking out. Pill popping? Are you kidding me? This was very hard to swallow, pun intended (great minds think alike!). It scared the crap out of me. Again, my deal breakers from day one were alcohol, drugs, and cigarettes. This was Strike 2 (considering the circumstances, I'm genuinely sorry for the baseball reference, Douglas, but I can't help myself).

When I heard this story, my defense mechanism to flee was instantaneous. Drugs and addiction was a huge part of the reason my life had been a living hell during my teens and early twenties. But thinking about the psychologist's words of wisdom, I was able to talk myself out of it. I decided to make a mental note and let it go. Doug said he conquered this problem and I chose to believe him. Also, I knew that he had never been so vulnerable before in a relationship. He'd always just had fun and never fully given all of himself. This was the first time he shared his feelings, without being forced to, and I knew it was a turning point with us. He trusted me with his deepest darkest secret and I'd never felt closer to him. We were going to fight our demons together.

But back to six weeks after we started the crazy experiment. It was time for "Decision Day." Were we going to stay together or split up? In the cab ride over to film the big finale, my stomach was doing summersaults and my heart was beating out of my chest. Doug was 100 percent certain but I was still 50/50, only because he'd just gained my trust back from the cigarette lie. Before we went in front of the camera, I told him, "Do not ever lie to me again." He promised he wouldn't. Doug also reiterated that if we broke up, we'd always regret not trying to make it work without cameras in our faces. "The thought of 'what if' would be worse than if it didn't work out," he said. "If we never give it a shot in real life, there will always be that 'what if.'"

"If we parted ways no one would care," I told him. "But if we continue, one of us might get hurt."

"Any relationship you get into that's a possibility," he answered.

It was getting down to it. The entire time I'd never had any intention of backing out of the experiment but now I had a real choice to make that was even more life-changing—commit further or bail. The scaredy-cat in me wanted to run like the wind. But the fact that we were legally married made it so much more difficult to give up. And made it so much more important to keep going. We made a commitment to each other. It was so much more profound than leaving a relationship where we're just dating. Surprisingly, Doug was a really good match. Was he too good of a match to up and leave?

The psychologist asked the million-dollar question. "We've come to the end of the experiment. Jamie and Doug, have you come to a decision? Are you going to stay married? Or are you going to get divorced?"

Doug answered first.

"My answer is absolutely yes. I choose to stay married."

My turn. Gulp.

"Like I said before, I don't take any of this lightly," I started. "It's such a big deal, it's a huge moment. It's so emotional." I paused for dramatic effect but not on purpose. "Ultimately you make me so comfortable and I hope we can fall in love and stay married and have babies. That perfect little family because that's what I want. So my answer is yes, I want to stay married."

We may be the only married couple to wait two months before consummating our marriage. After the show was over, we had to move out of our apartment and back into my place and real life as Mr. and Mrs. Hehner started. It wasn't a huge adjustment. Other reality dating shows rarely work because it puts couples in over-the-top fairy-tale scenarios and then expects them to plunge a toilet together afterwards. We'd already plunged a nasty toilet— true story—and dealt with other uncomfortable real-life scenarios. We had kept working our full time jobs throughout filming. While filming we had the busiest schedules. When the cameras finally went away, our relationship didn't fall apart. It got better.

Doug and I fell for each other all over again.

We were working opposite schedules—Doug 9 to 6 and me on the night shift from 7p – 7:30 am—yet our love skyrocketed. At 3 a.m. when I was on my break, he'd surprise me at the hospital with snacks and coffee. My coworkers loved him for this. He never complained that I had to sleep like a vampire until 4 p.m. and he left me sweet notes and gifts. He was always so thoughtful. For example, I loved his pillow so he bought me the same one, because it was $50 and he knew I'd never spend that much money on a pillow. We threw romantic monthly anniversary parties (we still do this today). We'd come so far and we wanted to celebrate us.

One muggy summer night, about a month after the experiment ended, Doug and I decided to stay in and hang in our bedroom, the coldest room in my apartment. We sat on the bed, drinking wine and playing Monopoly. Doug was kicking my butt and I was really annoyed because I hate losing. We were flirting and being playful, and the chemistry just built and built until it was about to explode.

"Are you sure?" he asked gently.

Doug pulled back. He didn't say, "Yes! Finally!" He'd waited for what seemed like a million years to do this and in the million and first year, he was still willing to not go all the way. Doug never ever pressured me. He never made me feel like less of a woman or wife for not consummating our marriage sooner. After everything we'd been through, I finally trusted that he respected me and wouldn't leave me. I know this sounds crazy but my mom didn't teach me about sex. All she told me was that "all men are the same. They only want one thing. A piece of ass. They'll love you and leave you." I believed her. I watched it happen to her over and over again.

I needed to know ten times over that Doug loved, respected and cared for me. I was finally there and he said, "Are you sure?" Nothing was a bigger turn-on. Doug was not just a horny man. He was a horny man who *loved me*.

Game over.

Okay, now for the good part. Everyone always wants to know, "Was it good? How was it?"

I wish I could say that our first night making love was fireworks exploding and magical and blissful and all-night long. Truth: It was hot and heavy for five minutes. I'm saying five minutes for Doug. It's okay, Doug laughs and jokes about it, too.

You know what? I wasn't disappointed—I was flattered because it meant that he was so into me! And I was so steamed up, I had an orgasm even though it was so short. The next morning we did it again and this time it was everything I'd hoped it'd be. We were like wild bunnies and it was super awesome. The waiting had been 100% worth it.

I used to have to be drunk to suffer through awkward, dispassionate sex. Now, I was truly making love with my best friend. And having, like, five orgasms. Doug and I have a routine going where we can actually have an orgasm simultaneously.

Please don't hate me! Be happy for me. For us.

CHAPTER 7

Making Good With The M.I.L.

Y ou know who wasn't happy for us? At all? It's not hard to guess. Doug's mother, Bonnie. I don't blame her. I made a horrible first impression at the wedding, especially when I made it crystal clear I wasn't attracted to her son by crying like a baby the second I laid eyes on him. I barely spoke to Bonnie or their family at the reception, avoiding any and all interaction like the plague, probably because I was in shock. Also, Bonnie is intimidating, the type of woman who makes her presence in a room known. She wasn't what I'd call a "wallflower" at the wedding. I was terrified of her. The first thing I remember about her was that she screamed out in disgust at Doug's choice of footwear right after we said our vows.

"I can't believe you wore those white shoes!"

I thought, who is this lady? Note to my younger self: That, my dear, is your new mother-in-law.

Like most moms would, she instantly went into Mama Bear mode and was protective of her cub. Bonnie, who grew up solidly middle class and comfortable, must have taken one look across the aisle and had a silent heart attack that this rude redneck girl and her family were now legally bound to her son.

At first, I didn't think to care what Bonnie thought because I never thought in a million years that the Hehners would be my "forever family." I made a lot of mistakes in this whole thing but that was a biggie. I had no intention of falling in love with Doug so I didn't realize that I'd set a very dangerous precedent—that his mother had good reason to reject me and this whole experiment.

In the middle of our honeymoon, when the tide turned and I decided I really liked him, the gravity of my lack of interactions with my new in laws hit me, and my stomach dropped. "Oh my God, your mom hates me," I told Doug. Of course I really wanted her to like me and think highly of me, but I'd messed up majorly, possibly permanently. I could have shown a lot more interest and excitement the day of our wedding but I felt paralyzed by my actions. What kind of first impression is that?

"She doesn't hate you, she just wants to get to know you," Doug explained sweetly.

Doug's words of encouragement did nothing to settle my nerves. After we got back, it was unavoidable and inevitable. We had to go see his family. It was the first time I'd see where he grew up and lived just prior to marrying me. It'd be the first time I saw his family after the wedding. We drove 90 minutes down to his parents' house in south Jersey, and I was so nauseous, I literally thought I might throw up. I wanted to bring a little gift of flowers or chocolates or something similar. We stopped by the mall and after going back and forth throughout the mall I opted for some fancy chocolate covered pretzels and strawberries to say thanks for welcoming me into their home.

When we got there, I offered my gift, as a sort of olive branch.

"Great, I'm diabetic," his sarcastic dad, Doug Sr., said. Failed attempt number one.

Sure enough, Bonnie didn't just lay down the red carpet for me. Don't get me wrong (or into more trouble!), she was polite, because she's a classy woman, but she did not take it easy on me or give me a break. In fact, while we were away, she'd discovered that I'd been on *The Bachelor*, and, if possible, it was all even worse now.

Doug Sr., Bonnie, Doug's brother Matthew and his fiancé, Kerri, were all there, so we went into the living room, one of those fancy middle class living rooms that had a plushy flower couch and smelled like fresh pine candles. After a few seconds of pleasantries,

Bonnie pointed her finger at me and transformed into Mariska Hargitay on *Law & Order: SVU*.

"What is your interest in this?" she flat out demanded. "I know about your dating history on *The Bachelor*."

I was being judged as to whether or not I was appropriate for their beloved firstborn. "I genuinely want to get married and have children," I told her. Bonnie looked at me like I had ten heads and she wasn't even about to take me seriously.

Suddenly shy and self-conscious, I pushed on, stuttering out an explanation for that terrible reaction I had at the altar. "I just looked down the aisle and couldn't see straight," I stammered. "I felt like I was marrying a monster."

"A MONSTER?!" Bonnie looked at me with disgust.

Failed attempt number two. I've never been very good with my words. Or maybe I'm just too honest. I deserved this.

It was clear from her line of questioning that she didn't think I was genuine. After I got my butt handed to me on a platter, thankfully, Doug's sister-in-law Kerri came to my rescue.

"We all have history," she reminded Bonnie.

It wasn't Kerri's job to defend me, and it was true that I did do all of that stuff and embarrass myself. But the gesture was greatly appreciated. It didn't help much though. Bonnie was still skeptical and would remain that way until I earned back her trust. Fair enough.

Here's the thing: If you know me by now, I never back down from a challenge, even (especially) one as tough as this. It's hard enough when your mother-in-law *does* like you. I'd dug a very deep hole that getting myself out of would be nearly impossible. But the stakes were too high for me to just give up. This was my marriage, my future. I was beginning to have deep feelings for her son and I didn't want any issues with my new in-laws—especially my Mother In Law. I really wanted that happy, welcoming family to be a part of.

Come hell or high water, I was going to win Bonnie over and prove that I genuinely cared about Doug and their family. She'd see that this was not a game to me, it was real. Here's how I did it, and hopefully if you have M.I.L. issues this will be helpful for you too!

1. *I found other allies in the family*

Bonnie was understandably distrustful of me, but I will say, I clicked immediately with Doug's dad, Doug Sr., who is very laid back and easygoing. Part of that might be due to the standard M.I.L. tension but I wonder if it had anything to do with the fact that Doug Sr. and I had a little more in common. We both grew up without dads around. His mother, Dot, was pregnant with two kids when their father (I hesitate to use that word) just up and walked out of their lives forever. Like me, Doug Sr. chose to try to break the chain and succeeded. He was, and is, the rock of the Hehner family. He was, and is, a provider and a protector, and totally involved in his children's lives, including coaching many of Doug's baseball teams.

I also got along swimmingly with Grandma Dot, who wasn't just a sweet little old Granny. Doug's grandmother was a spitfire, who didn't mince words. She was kind of blunt, like she'd tell one of her grandchildren, "You're getting fat!" I grew very close to Grandma Dot. I felt like she was the first Hehner who genuinely rooted for and supported our marriage. She was the first Hehner to truly accept and love me. I could see it and *feel* it. It meant the world to me. When Grandma Dot became bedridden in a hospital upstate, not far from where I grew up, I'd stop by on my drive to see my family. Sometimes I'd even go by myself. Grandma Dot liked that I was a nurse and we really enjoyed each other's company. She passed away last summer and I'm so grateful I got to know her for a very short time. We had such an unexplainable bond.

I drove up to see Grandma Dot a few times with Doug Sr. and we got really close on those trips. So close that Bonnie noticed I confided in her husband a lot and would try to pry info out of him about me.

"Come with and you can talk to her yourself!" Doug Sr. joked.

Early on, Bonnie and I tried to have a girls' day together by ourselves, taking my dog Lady to the groomer and having lunch, but it was too soon and really awkward. That was going to take more time. My relationship with Bonnie truly started getting better once she noticed that Doug confided in me and Grandma Dot was a big fan. Then slowly, once she saw that I wasn't a total ogre, our bond grew.

2. *I knew my role*

Doug only has one mother and it's Bonnie. I remember one time, we were all together, and he overslept. I had been trying to wake him up but he wasn't budging. It was frustrating and embarrassing for *me* because we all couldn't do anything or go anywhere until he got up. So I did what any sane person would do. I left him there and went upstairs to meet with the rest of the family. Everyone asked, "Where's Doug?" as if they didn't know he was sleeping. I had already complained that I had tried to wake him up and he wasn't moving.

"Go tell your husband to wake up!" Bonnie instructed me.

I looked straight at her.

"I am not his mother. He is a grown man." There's only so much I can do. I do not want to "mother" my husband.

Tell you what, she really respected me after that and never hounded me again to get him to do things. I'm Doug's W-I-F-E and I want it to stay that way.

On the flip side, I had to get used to the fact that Doug would always turn to his mom, not me, for certain things and there was nothing I could do about that but accept it.

3. *I was more open*

A big reason why it was so difficult for me to mesh with Bonnie is that I wasn't used to having a mother (or father) in the traditional sense. Meaning a mother and father who actually cared about what was happening in my life. So when Bonnie was overly involved in our lives or peppered me with questions, it took me some time to figure out that just going with it was way easier than fighting it or trying to be more private. I think it's just her way of showing she cares. Bonnie would ask everything from, "How's everything going?" to "Have you finished your taxes yet?" In my head I'd be steaming, like, I'm an adult! (Secretly I'd be thankful for the reminders.) I'm not used to having parents asking, "Are you doing this or are you doing that?" When Doug and I were looking at new homes to rent, Bonnie and Doug Sr. came with us, which was fine, but we disagreed about which house we all liked better and I felt outnumbered. They liked the house we are in right now because it was cleaner, closer to the city, newer and a better price. Turns out they were right but I just wasn't used to making decisions by committee. I was a one-woman show for a really long time. Then after we decided on our new New Jersey house, Bonnie said, "Did you get the down payment done?" It's strange to get this "questioning" because I'm so used to being independent. Rather than seeming like it came from a loving place it seemed like they didn't trust that we are mature and responsible enough to handle our business. Or maybe I was just overthinking it because I have NO IDEA how to handle a parental figure truly caring about these seemingly trivial tasks. She was just trying to make sure everything was done right. It came from a good place, but I just wasn't used to it. I've never had to kind of check back in with parents.

But that's irrelevant. Because to be in this family, I'd have to be more of an open book.

4. But not too open

In the beginning, I felt almost obligated to confide in Bonnie to build a strong bond. Someone once told me that your mother-in-law doesn't have to know everything. And shouldn't. For instance, and I know this is sort of a stereotype so don't bite my head off, but a lot of guys aren't very good about keeping in contact with their mothers and updating them about their lives. This includes Doug. Bonnie wanted to be very involved in his life and would complain that she'd have to read about his goings on in Facebook posts. Since he was a bit MIA, she saw me as the magic pipeline to retrieve more information. I quickly learned this was not a great idea. It's up to Doug when, how, where to upload info about his personal life. I once told Doug's parents about him not doing so well at work because he was stressed and behind. Bad idea. He was upset because he didn't want them to know. It got Doug and I into a huge argument and it didn't even bring Bonnie and I closer anyway. Pointless.

Another example, it was clear to me after just a few convos that Bonnie was stridently pro-life. So I definitely would not feel comfortable telling her about my past, and I didn't feel a burning desire to get into a heated argument about politics. I was certain if she knew about my abortions she'd go back to hating me and she'd definitely judge me. We were on opposite sides of the spectrum and weren't going to change each other's minds.

On that note, one question that Bonnie asked frequently was, "When are you going to get pregnant?" She was sort of joking but serious enough that I felt pressured.

"I'm the mother-in-law, I'd know first obviously," she said.

Sensitive subject here. Let's just say that I agree she will be one of the first to know and that's because she cares to know. It's nice to know she's excited to be a grandmother to our children and she can't wait to spoil them. I am happy to let her be the first to know—along with my sisters! My family is important, too.

5. I simply showed up

It felt weird to be part of a real family, who showed up for each other, but I faked it until I maked it! Whenever possible, I accepted an invite to Bonnie's house or other family activities. When I already had plans, I canceled or rearranged my schedule. When Doug didn't feel like it, I convinced him it was in our best interest. After Grandma Dot died, the family was going to meet for dinner. Doug refused to go, and after an argument, it came out that he was too sad and didn't want to have to fake being strong in front of everyone. I told him that his family needed him and he might find comfort with them. We ended up going and I know Bonnie was grateful we made it.

The only time my strategy of just showing up was difficult was when Bonnie wanted us to come to church every Sunday. I love church—it saved my life. When we have kids, I want to go back to church regularly. But right now, every Sunday is just not feasible with our schedule. Bonnie was adamant that we go on Christmas, so we went. And guess what, it felt good to see her smile and be genuinely happy on Christmas Eve—just because we showed up! I totally understand that feeling!

I was rewarded for my efforts—I started getting invited to the exclusive ladies' brunch tradition, with Bonnie, Doug's sister and his brother's fiancée Kerri and her mom, Linda. It felt really nice to be included. It felt like I was part of the family for real.

6. I adapted

Relationships are all about compromise. Same holds true when you're being initiated into a new family. Families are like snowflakes—no two are alike. You're not the priority, so you can't just go in there guns blazing and change dynamics that are decades in the making. If you want to fit in, you have to be a chameleon. This can be challenging.

As I've mentioned, I'm kind of a prude and a goody-goody. So it took a little time getting used to the Hehner dinner table, in which "shitting" is a main topic of conversation, Bonnie laughs so hard, she pees (literally ha!), and Doug's sister Lyndsay spits out her food. It was odd enough for me simply to be sitting around a table with an entire family. I grew up standing at the kitchen counter eating, or eating from fast food bags while driving home, so to sit down for any length of time was foreign to me. It wasn't often my family had dinners at the table together.

One of the biggest adjustments I had to make was spending the holidays with the Hehners. "Holidays with the Hehners" sounds like a special on The Disney Channel where they'd all wear ugly Christmas sweaters sitting around a fireplace singing carols! Anyway, the holidays in my family have always been hit and miss. We may have had a Christmas tree and gifts but there was no guarantee my mom would be there. She'd always get us presents from the cops or Toys for Tots. One year my mom forgot to pick up the toys, but they delivered them to our house anyway. When she opened the door, she told the cop some sob story and he must have felt so bad because he gave her a $50 bill from his own pocket.

After he left, Mom shut the door and yelled with glee, "I can't believe he just gave me 50 bucks!"

"Wow! Me neither! That's awesome!" I said. I was so happy we could get the younger kids gifts. They still believed in Santa. Mom needed help wrapping Christmas presents so me and my older sister Joh were clued in pretty early.

"Now I can get Lee that leather vest he really wanted!"

Say what? Lee was Mom's boyfriend at the time.

"Do not spend that money! That is not for him!"

We got in a big fight but she ended up getting Lee the leather vest.

I can't imagine this scenario at the Hehners. I can't picture Bonnie not calling her children on their birthdays or not seeing them on Thanksgiving. My first Thanksgiving with Doug's family was as cookie cutter as it comes, except for when my mom, who was so graciously invited, didn't show up and I cried. Of course I went upstairs to the bathroom to hide my crying. I didn't want the Hehners to think I was less than excited to have their company. (I always kick myself for even caring if my mom shows up or not. It's been years and years of her promising to be there and then randomly not showing up. I should be used to it now. But, can you ever really get used to it?) I had a wonderful time with my sisters and the Hehners, but it was also so weird and emotional for me. For Christmas, the Hehners had a big beautiful tree with stacks of presents underneath it. All of their children were there with their significant others and one person played Santa and passed out the gifts. For the past few years in my family, I always got the tree and the presents because if I didn't, there might not be any. I was always Santa and passed out all the gifts I'd bought. That was just kind of my thing so it was bizarre to just be the kid and sit there and have gifts passed out to me. It felt awkward to just sit and wait to be given presents.

I felt really self-conscious but you know what I did to make it normal? The woman who does my eyelashes is from Korea and didn't have family to celebrate with. I asked if she could come and Bonnie said yes. That's the cool thing about my in-laws. They are like, "The more the merrier!" I always feel more normal by taking the attention off myself and helping someone else. It makes me feel less awkward and more normal. So she came to our very first Christmas together and it was awesome.

7. I let go

With the Hehners, I might not be Santa and I also wasn't automatically going to be Princess Plan-A-Lot. Once, the entire family was going on vacation to the Outer Banks of North Carolina. In my world, I was always the boss—the one who picked out the activities and restaurants and paid for everything—so this time, it was uncomfortable when someone else was in charge. All I had to do was give our payment, everything else was arranged by Bonnie. It's hard for a Type A maniac like me to take a backseat but somehow I did it. Bonnie didn't want my input on which house or where we were going.

8. I chose my battles wisely

If you're in this for the long haul, getting your panties in a wad at every little thing will make your life miserable. I had to learn to just let certain things go because they just weren't that important in the grand scheme of things. Like, paying dinner tabs. My in-laws always want to pay for everything. I used to embarrassingly fight Bonnie to cover the tab just because I felt bad that she was always paying for everything. But she legit gets angry if I even try to sneak around and pay. I am not one who can sit back and just say "thank you" and smile. I feel like I have to show my appreciation and just a thank you and a smile isn't enough. Otherwise I feel like I am taking advantage of them and I owe them. But instead of fighting Bonnie at every bill I have learned to show my appreciation and pay them back in another way. So, instead, I plan on giving her "thank you" presents. Just to show my appreciation and not get her angry in the meantime. Because that is so not worth it. She can't complain about a thank you gift. :-D And in the meantime I'm trying to just enjoy people being so nice and giving to me instead of fighting them because it feels awkward and like I owe them for it. That isn't fair.

9. I didn't mix family politics

Blending two families together can be a seamless dream (NOT!) or a scary hideous disaster (picture me raising my hand). I mean, Bonnie saw my tears at Thanksgiving when my mom blew us off. I'm not used to showing that kind of vulnerability publicly, and I'd never in my life subjected my partner and his family to our special blend of drama and dysfunction. But when you're married, you almost have no choice in the matter. There will be events where families are going to cross-pollinate whether you like it or not. I wish ours could blend, I want my siblings to be part of the Hehners. Heck, I even want my mom to be part of the Hehners.

For Doug's and my one-year anniversary, we renewed our vows in St. Thomas and invited our immediate families. This would be the longest the Hehners would spend with my mom, plus on a vacation? Heck, this was the longest *I* had spent with my mom. This had catastrophe written all over it. I was so stressed that Bonnie would judge my mom but oddly, I was the one who ended up feeling more misunderstood. One morning my mom just didn't come down to breakfast. I was obviously used to this kind of thing.

"Shouldn't you let her know that breakfast is going to end soon?" Bonnie asked.

"She'll come down when she's ready," I said.

"You should really let your mom know," Bonnie said to me with an adamant look in her eyes.

I went up and let my mom know like a good little girl, but I wanted to say, feeling offended, "You can let her know if you're that worried about it."

I'd opened up to Bonnie about my mom but I definitely felt like she didn't understand my situation with my mother. Her only response was a sharp, flat, "You only have one mom."

That is true but that doesn't mean I can endlessly forgive and forget the hurtful things my mom has done to me and my siblings over and over again. Don't tell me to take care of and look after my mom. My mom and I have a very rough relationship. I love my mom to death and I'll be the first to defend her if someone is being mean and judgmental towards her, but my issues with my mom are still at the forefront of my mind. She has burned my siblings and me so many times in so many different ways. Yes, I only have one mom. Yes, I need to forgive. But these things take time. They are slowly resolving.

I told Doug how upset I was after Bonnie and my conversation, but all he offered was, "She didn't mean it. You're being too sensitive."

This trip was not the romantic getaway I dreamed of. Doug and I had been working so hard for the past ten months, basically speed dating each other to catch up, and I don't know that we were 100 percent on the same page. Let alone the same room. The day after we renewed our vows, Doug went water skiing all day with the guys, while I hung with Bonnie and Kerri. I tried pretending I didn't care, but deep down inside I wanted my husband to CHOOSE to spend all of his time with me on our vow renewal—not go goof around with the guys. To make matters worse, he didn't even sit next to me at dinner, his dad did. I just felt so far from him rather than close to him. Maybe it was selfish of me, but I had hoped my hubs would want to spend every moment with me celebrating our vow renewal. Instead I felt like he was a kid who just got unleashed at Disney and I had to chase him down to catch up with him.

For the rest of the trip, I limited my own time with both Mom and Bonnie together until I could figure out how to manage Bonnie's insistence that I treat my mom like my "mom." For my sanity and the health of my marriage. She clearly doesn't understand the dynamics and doesn't seem to care to try and understand either.

10. *I accepted love*

Everything mentioned so far are normal situations so many daughters and mothers-in-law experience. I can't stress enough that despite a few trying times, Doug's mother showed me a love I'd never experienced before, even though we're not even blood related.

When Doug and I finally moved into our home in New Jersey, she and Doug Sr. *gave* me their car, a Chrysler 200, to borrow until I could get my own. I was speechless, my brain froze. I didn't even know how to say thank you because nobody had ever done anything that generous for me before without taking it back and making my life a living hell. Cough cough, my grandmother. It's hard for me to accept gifts because I'm scared they will be used against me later on in life. Because of this I always feel like I owe someone.

When I first became part of the Hehner clan, I didn't even know the right etiquette to be a caring, considerate family member. One day immediately after I got out of work I was supposed to drive down to visit Bonnie and Doug Sr., but I was so tired from my night shift, I dropped Doug off at work (we were sharing his car at the time) and pulled into the back parking lot to rest my eyes because they were stinging. I felt like I just couldn't keep them open long enough for the 45-minute drive down to his parents. I fell asleep and showed up several hours late without calling. In my family, that was status quo but Doug's parents were sick, just beside themselves with worry. That was a foreign concept to me. Someone actually noticed that I was missing? Now, Bonnie always says to me, "Get home safe!" and that's so sweet but I'm still not used to it.

I'm not sure I'll ever get used to Bonnie telling me, "I love you" when we're leaving or getting off the phone. Doug and I didn't even say it to each other until six months after we were married. I don't know why I freeze up when someone says they love me. Or if I go to say it to someone for the first time. It's not like I never heard it growing up. My mom always told me she loved me. She still does. I guess that is partially the problem. Just because someone says they love you, doesn't mean they truly love and care about you. I'm not saying my mom doesn't, but she has a funny way of showing it sometimes. I just get so uncomfortable with it all, I just avoid it altogether.

Bonnie recently started saying it to me a lot after conversations. I never say it back, because I'm weirded out by it. "Ahhh, have a good night!" I'll say back, stuttering and sputtering. I do love them but I almost feel like saying it will be a jinx. It's a thing that you want so bad and when you have it you're shy about it, maybe because you're scared it might go away. At least for me. It's almost like I don't want to rock the boat. If it's there, just be happy it's there and don't mention it.

So that's how I wormed my way back into Bonnie's heart after an inauspicious start. I'll never forget the first compliment my mother-in-law ever gave me because it was the best kind.

"Doug's so happy," she said. "I'm so happy that he's happy."

I was so happy that she was happy. I didn't have the heart to tell her that I wasn't sure Doug and I were happy anymore.

There are some things your mother-in-law doesn't need to know. And shouldn't.

CHAPTER 8

Attack Of The Lovers' Spats

D oug and I had a blink-and-you'll-miss-it honeymoon—sadly our honeymoon period was over before we knew it, too. No one *wants* their honeymoon period to be over, but it's unrealistic to expect it to last forever. Ours was a bit too short and semi-sweet. We experienced pure bliss from about six months in, after cameras stopped rolling, to our vow renewal. During this time, we were so head-over-heels, we could do no wrong in each other's eyes, even in the worst of times. I got really sick—hacking cough like consumption, blowing nose louder than a foghorn—and Doug wasn't grossed out by me at all. I told him I wanted to sleep downstairs on the couch so I could prop myself up and not bother him as I drowned in my own phlegm. He not only set up a cozy couch for me and bought me a heating pad, he slept next to me to make sure I was okay. I didn't ask him to and he didn't have to. I'm usually a very independent woman, but I turn into a big baby and super needy when I'm sick. Nobody ever took care of me before. My husband stepped up. Vice versa, when Doug is asleep, he's a big drooler, but I didn't even mind when I'd roll over in bed and my cheek would land in a puddle of his gook. Ok, if I'm being completely honest I do get a bit grossed out by this—I mean c'mon I'm only human. But I just wipe it off my face and give him a loving peck on the forehead. He can't help his drooling.

Certain things that easily make other couples go sideways were seamless for us. I loved his family. We both loved each other's friends. Neither of us cared if we didn't make the bed in the morning. Crucially, we were completely on the same page about social media.

Social media can be a nightmare/torture for anyone going through a breakup, but it can equally wreak havoc on a marriage. There's the basic issue of paying more attention to your phone than your spouse. Doug and I did not have that problem. Probably because he's more fixated on watching TV than tooling around on his phone. I'm definitely guiltier in this situation, my head down answering emails, texts and comments from my followers. But neither of us found it that intrusive in our relationship and we had a steadfast rule that during dinner, phones are turned off so the only conversation we had was with each other.

Another pothole can be the whole password situation. Does your spouse know your password to your phone, emails, etc? And is he/she allowed to go on your phone at any time? For Doug and I, the answer was yes to both of those questions. We did know each other's codes and we were allowed to look for anything we wanted. But neither of us ever actually checked the other's phone. In my opinion, demanding to tear into Doug's phone meant "I don't trust you" and I wanted no part of that. I didn't want to live like that. If we needed to see each other's phone that meant to me that we were on the brink of divorce because if you don't have trust then you have nothing.

I'm not really a jealous person and I was confident that Doug was not cheating on me, in real life or on social media. Despite the fact that women love my husband and weren't shy about posting it for the entire universe to see. Hot little Barbie commenters, as I dubbed them, bombarded Doug with public pleas to dump me and hook up with them from the very start on Instagram, Twitter, and Facebook.

"Run, Doug!"

"She doesn't deserve you!"

"She needs therapy!"

"You can do better!"

Yes, people actually leave these comments and tweets. This obviously is really hurtful to read over and over again. I wasn't *worried*, though. I knew Doug only had eyes for me, even if I wasn't the "best" wife. Doug ignored those little Barbies. Yes, he was on a TV show, but he didn't crave or need attention. He loves the fans but he's not addicted to the attention from social media. In fact, if I did see him on there a lot, it'd be a red flag. If suddenly his head was hunched over his phone, I'd think, "Who's grabbing his attention?" On the flip side, he wasn't worried about me either. Guys never hit on me on social media, plus, Doug's attitude about it was, "Go ahead! You deal with her mood swings!"

My mood swings. His moodiness. We'd been on our absolute best behavior for nine months, but slowly, I can't pinpoint an exact time, the screws came loose and the wheels fell off the cart. The more we got to know each other, the more our real personalities surfaced and we fought about our differences.

Some fights were silly, like about loading the dishwasher.

Phase 1: It's early in the relationship, so Doug is really conscientious about picking up after himself and eager to load the dishwasher.

Phase 2: Getting more comfortable in the relationship, Doug contracts amnesia and doesn't know how to place items in said dishwasher. Knives go in blade up. Plates go in crusted with cheese and dried-up ranch dressing. Cups go in face up, thereby filling with dirty water and other food particles that have been flying around during the cycle, such as said cheese or perhaps noodles.

Phase 3: Full-blown in the relationship, Doug thinks the dishwasher has disappeared completely. If I don't load the dishwasher, we will not have clean dishes or silverware, and will have to eat with our fingers like we're at the Medieval Times restaurant.

We are still in Phase 3.

When the bloom comes off the rose, compromise becomes an endangered species. Take deciding what to have for dinner every night. At first, I happily ingested Doug's frozen food treats because I wanted to make him happy. But eventually, I needed to eat real food for my own sanity and couldn't take one more sodium-infused, Frankenstein-created bagel bite. This is the argument we'd have. I know I'm not alone in this one:

"What do you want for dinner?"

"I don't care, you pick."

"A cheeseburger."

"No, I want healthy."

"You decide then!"

"How about chicken Francese?" One of his favorite meals (fyi: just because it has chicken doesn't mean it's good for you).

"What do *you* want?"

"Sushi."

"*Not* sushi. Anything but sushi."

Doug's tolerance for sushi lessened as time went on, as did my tolerance for Howard Stern. Doug is obsessed with the so-called King of All Media and he's all Doug listens to in the car. Driving with

Doug is a challenge. Number one, he drives way too fast and way too close to the cars in front of him. Number two, he can't go a day without listening to Howard Stern without feeling intense FOMO (fear of missing out). When we first got married, he could tell I was having anxiety attacks when he drove like a maniac and chivalrously slowed down to a grandmotherly pace just for me. In return, I suffered through Howard Stern asking porn stars how many times per day they masturbate and make bowel movements. But now Doug ignores my pleas to slow down and I will only listen to Howard's interviews with celebrities because they're usually not quite as vulgar. In my car, it's my choice—CNN or Fox News or podcasts like *Serial*. Doug thinks those are boring. If we listen to music, I like country, he likes music from his high school and college days, like Sublime. Don't tell Doug I secretly call them Sublame in my head.

No, these are not serious issues. These are just universal things every couple deals with on a daily basis in one form or another that didn't seriously threaten to tear us apart. But Doug and I did have some "real" problems that surfaced from the beginning, the kind of issues that study after study shows are major indicators of future divorce—arguments about money, sex, and communication.

Here are some sobering stats:

- Money is still the number one source of conflict for married couples and the number one reason for divorce, even over infidelity.

- Couples who argued about money early in their relationships—regardless of their income, debt or net worth—were
at a greater risk for divorce, according to a Kansas State
University study.

- Couples who disagreed about money once a week were 30
percent more likely to get divorced than couples who argued
about it once a month, a Utah State University study found.
Also interesting, wives were more likely to get divorced over
finances and sex, but for husbands, fights about money were
the only arguments that predicted whether they would get
divorce. Thank God, because by now we know the sex for
Doug was hit or miss with me.

Oh goody gumdrops. Doug and I fought about all of that. I
knew we would have issues about money literally from the moment
I met him and the first thing that came out of his mouth was that
he lived with his parents at the age of thirty-one. It's funny because
the experts did such a great job matching Doug and I up in almost
every area, except for this one very significant topic. Maybe it was
intentional and they were trying to balance us out, but it seems to me
they should have seen that our backgrounds and philosophies about
finances were diametrically opposed.

Doug grew up in a very comfortable, privileged middle class
family. We all know how I grew up. Doug had all of life's necessities
plus luxuries provided for him. I knew at a very young age, if I didn't
work, I might not have food, shelter or heat. Starting around the age

of eleven, I babysat kids in my neighborhood for peanuts, about $5 for an entire day. I was a saver from the very start. I remember once, we didn't have any milk or bread, and my mom had zero money. I'd stashed my birthday money safely in my piggy bank.

"I have $6, Momma!" I said proudly.

"No, that's yours, honey, you keep it," she said. She didn't take my money, even in the direst circumstance when I was younger (when I got a little older it was a different story).

When I was invited to friends' houses for dinner, I was always astonished how ungrateful the kids were. The moms had always bent over backwards to make dinner and these inconsiderate spoiled brats would complain that they wanted pizza for dinner instead. I'd wolf down whatever the mom had made, so thankful for a home-cooked meal.

At fourteen, I got a special permit to work after school at Arby's even though I was underage. I started bringing home Beef 'n Cheddars and french fries for my siblings. It felt amazing to see their faces light up when I'd walk in the door with food. I liked feeling like a bit of a hero. In my early days, I'd save up my money and buy myself a pair of designer jeans and the sense of accomplishment infused me with purpose and confidence. The older I got, and the more my mom started disappearing, my paychecks became less novelty, more necessity. But I'd already had a fire lit under my butt. I didn't need anyone or anything to motivate me.

I understood the value of a dollar before I probably needed to, but I was grateful I did. Along the way I learned lessons about money the hard way. I learned consequences. If I got a speeding ticket and just didn't pay it for a year (true story), it wouldn't magically go away, the fine would double. If I didn't pay the electric bill, not only would it be shut off, it'd cost $400 to turn it back on again. This I learned from my Momma.

I made every penny I did earn count. I went grocery shopping at two different stores to make sure I was getting the cheapest prices. If my gas tank was almost on empty, I'd put in $5 at the nearest gas station just so I could make it to the farther gas station that had lower prices. Believe me, I knew what it was like to be down to scrounging for change in my couch cushions and glove compartment so I could buy propane to heat our trailer.

These techniques were ingrained in my brain, and, ironically, it was my mother's words that influenced me most.

"Never rely on a man," she told me many times. Even though she was doing the exact opposite of what she said, I got it. It sank in. I wouldn't rely on a man—or her, or anyone. I would work my tail off so that I'd never have to worry again about food, heat, a home. And that's just what I did.

I truly believe that people who work hard are survivors. It's not an accident that I chose being a nurse over a teacher. Both teaching and nursing are very rewarding, but nursing is just about the most secure job there is. There will *never* not be a need for nurses. Even if all of the opportunities I've found in TV hosting and becoming an entrepreneur with jewelry making (my latest passions) go away, I will be able to work and provide for myself and my husband. And I'll always help my siblings but that doesn't mean I'll just make it rain willy-nilly. I learned early on that handouts don't work. Once, I loaned my sister $20 to get diapers and she promised to pay me back on Friday. Friday came and went, and nada. When I asked her to repay the money she owed me, she brought over a radar detector her boyfriend had stolen. Um, no thanks. I never loaned cash out again. Ever since, I'm a little slyer with my financial help. I give gift cards to grocery stores or Amazon, or I buy it as a "gift." When my younger sister was 16, she wanted a cellphone so badly. I saved my money up and bought her the phone.

I'm not trying to win a humanitarian award but I do enjoy spending my money on others before myself. There are very few things that I splurge on, other than good quality jewelry and a designer handbag once in a blue moon. I don't need a fancy car or $500 Louboutins. I actually just bought myself a winter coat for $120 and felt a little guilty because I have two other coats. Spending $120 on a coat is a lot to me when you already have two other ones hanging up in the closet but I splurged because I am so sick of spending winters in NYC/NJ FREEZING. This coat goes literally down to my ankles to keep me warm. I don't even care if I look like a granny walking down the street. At least I am warm!

Having said all that, it's no wonder that Doug and I fought the most about money. When I met Doug, he had almost just filed for bankruptcy. He'd owned a house with a friend but when they had to sell it during the recession, they lost $14,000 on it. He also was laid off from two jobs during this time. Unable to keep up with his bills, he stopped paying his credit cards and his credit score was destroyed.

He moved back home to start over. That's when his parents started paying his car loan and cellphone bill. A month before we were married he was hired at a great company called iCims as a software salesman. Supposedly he was paying them back, but I wasn't certain that was actually happening. This was very unattractive to me. We were working adults. His parents are retired.

"Why would you *want* them to do that?" I said disgusted. "Make sure you give them the money."

"Mind your own business."

Of course, I didn't mind my own beeswax. I had a really hard time letting go of this and the fact that he had absolutely no savings. How was I going to raise a family or buy a home with a man who wasn't financially sound? All I ever dreamed of was buying a house with stairs and a driveway. How would I be able to afford this with Doug as my husband? His credit was so bad; I'd have to get pre-approved for a house loan in my name only. The thought of having that tough responsibility solely on my shoulders was scary.

When I first met Doug's parents, his mom told me I should take control of his paycheck. I refused to do that. I didn't want that responsibility. I wanted him to be mature and take care of it himself. Wish I had listened to her advice!

Doug's money maturity level was pretty low and it annoyed me. While I'd go to the ends of the earth to get a bargain, Doug did his shopping at a QuickMart, which wasn't really a grocery store so they jacked up their prices. He was too lazy to drive farther to a real supermarket. I'd *never* do that. He'd pay six bucks for a box of cereal that cost four bucks at the grocery store five minutes down the road. He also spent about $20 per day on Starbucks coffee, bagels, and sandwiches. It didn't occur to him or he just didn't care that it added up.

I mentioned before that in my opinion, Doug is also a bit impulsive with his purchases and doesn't think about whether or not whatever he's buying is actually necessary. I raised an eyebrow when three big packages from Express came for him.

"Douglas, you don't need any more new clothes!"

I don't want to be like this but I can't help it. Doug wanted a new huge flat screen for our bedroom even though we already had a TV in there that worked fine. Well, knowing that I didn't approve, he went out and bought one anyway, then presented it as a "surprise" for me. "Isn't it great?" he said. No, it is not great. I was not happy about being "surprised," and furious that he bought such a big-ticket item without talking to me about it. Anytime I have to make a purchase worth a couple hundred dollars or more I always talk to him first. We need to save up for our first home.

If I henpecked Doug about his spending habits, or the fact that he ignored his credit card bills and they just sat there, it would cause an argument. Doug likes to be happy and have a good time, and dealing with depressing credit card balances didn't fit in that philosophy. So he threw it under the rug. I'm the opposite. I tackle things head on, bring it out in the open and take care of it.

From Doug's point of view, he thinks I need to calm down. He says he works hard and should be able to spend his money how he wants. Plus, he hates when I judge his financial relationship with his parents. He says just because it's different from my experience growing up doesn't make it bad. I see it all entirely differently. I'm a big saver. I see no reason to spend money unless we have to.

We were not on the same wavelength at all so we decided not to have a joint bank account and we still don't to this day. I don't know how much money he has exactly in his bank account and he doesn't know how much I have. I don't want to know. I want to trust my husband that he can manage his own money. I know this sounds naïve but it's how it has to be for our marriage to work. It's an extra stress on my shoulders that I don't want.

When we were living in NYC I paid all the bills and Doug just bought the groceries. Since moving into our new home in New Jersey, we switched. Now Doug pays the rent and I pay for groceries and utilities. This way, our finances are our own and that's the best way for us. My goal is to open up a joint savings account so we put in an equal amount each month. I'd feel more secure knowing we have a spending allowance but we haven't figured that out yet.

We are both trying to meet in the middle on the money matters. Doug wanted to buy a new car because his current car has over 100,000 miles. But I convinced him that it runs fine and we don't need a new car payment right now. At the same time, I've lessened my nitpicking and I don't count every penny he's spending. He's right, it's his hard-earned money and he can spend it how he likes. I continue to hold out hope that he's saving at least a little for our first home, our future, and our future Baby Hehners. (Yes, plural!)

I mentioned that I found Doug's immaturity not very hot. Unfortunately, that translated to the bedroom, where we were already having problems because of my deep-rooted issues. There was a time when our sex life was smoking hot but it was short-lived. And it's 100 percent my fault. The truth is I'm insecure about my body. I know I'm not repulsive or grotesque. It's not like I have boils on my skin. But I don't feel sexy and I'm embarrassed to be naked. I don't know why and it's a big problem.

If it were up to Doug, we'd be naked all the time. He wants skin on skin contact and I'm just not comfortable in the moment, still after all of this time. I can't let my head relax. I have to be reassured that he's not just getting into my pants, even though he's not like that at all. I don't know how to shut it off.

I should be excited when I'm in bed with him, but I have to work at being intimate with him all the time. It's the big elephant in the (bed)room. It's not that I'm not sexually attracted to him—he has the hottest body of any man I've ever been with. I'm just screwed up in the head. Can I blame it on my past? I don't know. What I do know is that thoughts of my ex kept creeping into my head. I'd always been so comfortable and adventurous with Stan. Why couldn't I be that way with Doug?

Doug and I didn't experiment the way we should, and I take full responsibility for that. It's not like we didn't have our passionate moments or fun with toys and oils. We even got this penis vibrating thing once but couldn't figure out how to turn it off. "Make it stop!" Doug screamed, laughing. By the way, I'm not big on the whole dress-up thing. It seems like spending hundreds of bucks at Victoria's Secret is a waste when it's just going to come off anyway! On the other hand, I'm 100 percent all for watching porn with your spouse. It's a sin but it's better than him looking at it alone, which he's going to do anyway. So let it go.

I don't know who I think I am asking you to let something go when I can't let go of certain things either. It's a little hypocritical (Geesh, there it is again—me being a hypocrite. I need to work on this!), especially because I know it's critical that I figure out my own shortcomings before it's too late. I worried about Doug leaving me for being unsatisfied with our sex life. I wouldn't blame him.

Doug and I should have talked about it but we were not the best at having serious, honest conversations. Like I said before, Doug likes to be happy and it made him uncomfortable to get into difficult discussions because he didn't know how to act or respond. I noticed that the only time we were able to go deep was on car rides we took together that were more than an hour long. And if we'd turned off Howard Stern.

Doug also gets his feelings out better in writing. After he went water skiing and ignored me at dinner during the vow renewal trip, he sent me an email apologizing:

I feel terrible and I'm sorry.

I got so wrapped up and completely frustrated with this trip, having both our families here, and how it became more of a little family vacation rather than a honeymoon. I wasn't there for you. I honestly didn't realize until you told me how distant I was. PLEASE come with me tomorrow and spend the rest of this trip together, just you and me. I have beach horseback riding planned, and I want to go to all the places we went on our first honeymoon—Coral World, the lift to Paradise Point.

I absolutely love you with all of my heart, and I love everything about you, and I'm sorry I made you feel that way. It's all my fault. I feel horrible.

None of those excursions ever happened.

Depends on which study you look at, but lack of communication can also be cited as the number one reason couples divorce. *YourTango.com* found that men name nagging as their top communication complaint, while women say it's not having their opinions validated.

Check. Doug definitely felt like I nagged or more specifically, that I pushed buttons that drove him crazy. Like, it really made Doug irate when I told him he was being juvenile or irresponsible. He hated how I would compare our marriage to my old relationship with Stan. (Duh!)

Check. I definitely felt a little ignored. Doug needed downtime to decompress, often going into his own world and not bringing me with him. I just wanted him to open up to me. Share what his feelings and thoughts were. I wanted to feel included in his little world, but I felt like I was an outsider.

About a year after we got married, I noticed a dramatic shift in our relationship. We were disconnected and on a downward spiral. For the first time, I felt like *Doug* was tired of putting in so much effort and had one foot out the door. My husband's best quality was that he was always willing to listen to constructive criticism, and had no problem apologizing if he realized he was wrong about something. He was open to working on himself and, unlike me, was not a grudge holder. But the man had limits.

Even though we were going through a hell of a time, I wanted to prove to Doug that I was committed to him and to our marriage. I finally legally changed my last name to Hehner for our one-year anniversary gift. I'd always wanted to take my husband's last name because of the shame associated with Otis. Here's a quick story on why I used to be so ashamed to be an Otis: The first time I met the man who I was named after was on the telephone. I was nineteen

JAMIE OTIS | Wifey 101

years old and my three younger siblings were living with me. Before my mom had left us to go be with her drug buddies she had been filing for child support from my little sister, AmyLynn's dad. First, she had to prove that this man was indeed her father. We will just call him Mr. Otis in this book. By the time the DNA tests came back positive and it went through the courts, AmyLynn was living with me and my mom was nowhere to be found. So, Mr. Otis called my cell phone looking for his newly determined daughter. Can you imagine how awkward the conversation was when Mr. Otis calls introducing himself and then asks who he is talking to? I reply that I am Jamie Otis and then quickly add, "I know you aren't my dad even though I have your last name. My little sister, AmyLynn, is your daughter. Here, let me get her for you...." Ever since that phone conversation I felt like Otis didn't really belong to me. Or I didn't belong to it.

Changing my last name to Hehner was such a joy for me. I was finally able to replace this random man's last name on the end of my name with a name that isn't random at all. I had finally found a man who loved me enough to stick with me through every single battle we encountered. What's better, I found a man who I wanted to stick with through every obstacle in life. Changing my last name to my husband's was a sign to Doug that I was (finally) willing to meet him halfway. That I knew I hadn't been a good wife and I hadn't tried my hardest but I was ready and willing to go there now. I was giving it one last shot with everything that I had.

Here's how the recovery to our marriage began: on our one-year anniversary we were hanging on by a thread. I had been impossible to please and he was fed up feeling like I compared him to my ex, Stan. He said he felt like he would never compare to Stan in my eyes. But just in good ol' Dougie fashion he decided to give our first anniversary everything he had. The difference was, this time so did I. Doug made reservations at a nice, local Italian restaurant. We had a candlelit dinner at a corner table. Doug gave me a beautiful set of diamond earrings and a matching necklace. I gave Doug a card that told him how much I loved him and showed him the confirmation number to a romantic ski trip in Vermont that I booked for us. Then I handed him a gift bag filled with some random "As seen on TV"— his favorite—items and at the very bottom of the bag was a itty-bitty box. Stuffed neatly inside the box was one single piece of paper that was from the social security office. On the top of the paper I wrote "I promise this isn't a positive pregnancy test." A baby is the last thing we needed in this rocky relationship. Doug couldn't push back the tears in his eyes as he unfolded the paper that read Jamie Nicole Hehner. I had completely surprised him by legally taking his last name. He immediately wrapped his arms around me and we gave each other the most loving hug. Doug said for the first time he felt like I was excited to be a Hehner and proud to be with him. But more than anything my unexpected attempt at getting Team Damie (the name we were dubbed) back on track was "comforting." With tears in my eyes I told him that I know I've been less than perfect as a wife and that I was sorry for having one foot out the door when he always had both feet planted on the ground. I thanked him for always staying by my side and never leaving me even though it's gotten really bad. I told him that I was going to work on me and our marriage. For the first time in our entire relationship I was truly going to give it my ALL.

But it was too little too late.

One day, we went fencing, as one of the activities on Doug's pre-baby bucket list. We weren't really having fun though. Out of the blue, Doug went deep.

"I'm doubting that we're right for each other," he said bluntly.

Whoa. Be careful what you wish for. This whole time I've been dying for him to share what was going on in his head when he retracted into his own little world. The minute he was honest about his feelings, I felt like a bulldozer crushed my heart. I felt vulnerable and exposed. Maybe I needed to feel that. I mean, that was exactly what I had been making Doug feel like on and off since the beginning of our marriage

The worst part of what he said? He wasn't wrong.

CHAPTER 9

Exes And Oh-No's

There was a third person in our relationship. No, we weren't having a ménage a trois, although maybe Doug would have liked that since our sex life definitely needed spicing up. After a brief honeymoon period in which we bonked like bunnies, I'd retreated back to old habits of being shy and distant in the bedroom. Ya know that saying "old habits die hard?" Yeah, I've realized there's nothing truer. Doug's habit of cutting me out of his life was on full force and even though I was making attempts to be a better wife (finally!) I still had a slew of issues to work on.

The first one being Stan. Without even knowing it, he was wreaking havoc in our relationship. It was clear that our marriage wasn't going to go from the brink of Divorceville to happily married over night. As a matter of fact, it got even worse.

Right after we renewed our vows, I went upstate to see my family and I also planned on attending one of Stan's shows at a local club. Doug was supposed to come with me—he'd agreed to meet my ex for the first time—but at the last second he blew it off. I figured if Stan and Doug could just meet they'd become friends quickly and it wouldn't be "strange" for me to remain in contact with an old flame. This may seem naïve of me, but my thoughts were basically, 'Why can't we all be friends?' Doug said he wanted to go and meet my ex. He told me that he wanted to get to know anyone that important in my life. That made me feel so loved and appreciated. But then at the last minute he claimed he had to work. It felt like a big ol' excuse. He probably didn't want to hang out with Stan, but frankly, he probably didn't want to hang out with my family either. After being a dutiful husband in the beginning, he'd pretty much stopped making the trek to my hometown altogether. It had been months since he took the time to go up and visit my family. It made me feel like he didn't give a crap about them at all. That really hurt.

I hadn't really seen much of Stan since Doug and I got married. But not long after I became Mrs. Hehner, I had to go to Stan's house to begin retrieving some of my belongings. (Yes, everything from my trailer was still being stored in his garage. And Yes, looking back now

I realize that seems a bit messed up.) But you wanna know what's more messed up? When I saw him, we hugged and I actually cried on his shoulder. I mean the tears were streaming down and the snot was ungracefully flowing out. All of my old feelings came back to the surface involuntarily. I felt like I had completely betrayed him by getting married and being happy, even though he never indicated that was true and he had a new girlfriend anyway. I kept thinking, "How does Stan feel about this?" I deeply cared for this man. I had always envisioned marrying *him* and having *his* babies. He was always so supportive and encouraging of me—even when I was crazy enough to marry a stranger. I felt like I just left him hanging.

Another time I went upstate to visit my family Stan and I ran into each other at the supermarket and chatted for a few minutes. My stomach had butterflies and my heart was jumping out of my chest. I wanted to stay longer. That meant I knew I couldn't see him anymore for a long time. I may be a lot of bad things but cheater isn't one of them. This was bad business. I felt conflicted, bummed out, and confused. I'd made a conscious choice to move on, but my heart was still with him. I had a desire to be near Stan, so I kept my distance. That wouldn't be fair to Douglas.

I made a vow to myself not to see him again, but that doesn't mean I didn't talk to him. During the first year of my marriage, I called Stan three to four times per week. Before you jump down my throat, in my defense, when I first signed up to do a "dating experiment," I didn't know I would end up married a month later. Stan and I were best friends, who had a deep connection and talked constantly up until I said, "I do." My old dog Kyla still lives at his house. The truth of the matter is, he was the first person to love me unconditionally. Not even my own mother has shown me a love like that. I've never been treated with such love and respect. How was I to just shut him out of my life immediately and completely when he was one of the only people in my life who always included me in his? It was excruciating to think about cutting him out of my life just because I am married now. It didn't seem fair to Stan, either.

I'll share more about what happened with Stan later, but before you crucify me, know that Doug invited the girl he lost his virginity to—still *his* best friend—to our wedding. I had no idea who she was when I met her and how important she'd been to him. She was happily married with two kiddos, so not even slightly a threat, but that's not the point.

The point is: We all have a past. You can't erase it. And sometimes your past is part of your present—and your future. This sounds like an Abbott and Costello "Who's on First?" sketch. At our wedding, I had no idea that Doug's first love was there and he had no idea that Stan helped create our wedding song. In fact, Doug made the joke, "I can't believe you picked this song! How did you know it's my favorite?" If he knew beforehand, would it have been a problem? Probably!

Doug didn't know about Stan until our honeymoon and, even after I spilled the beans, he didn't ask a lot of questions and didn't seem threatened. Doug is a very confident man and not a jealous person at all. We are similar like that. Growing up, I was jealous of the girls who had money and nice clothes and hot meals, but I've never been the type to be crazy possessive in a relationship. Doug confided to me that he'd had three major girlfriends before me.

1. The virginity girl, who is now a good friend of mine, too. I'm very glad I didn't pre-judge or ostracize her unnecessarily because she's awesome. She and Doug were friends in high school and both wanted to get rid of their v-cards so they experimented together to get it over with, with someone they trusted. Sounds smart and safe to me!

2. His college girlfriend, who is now also a nurse. One time, Doug Sr. had a fast heartbeat and had to go to the hospital. Well, this ex happened to be working at their local hospital and all of Doug's family was so happy to see her because they just loooooved her. I was at work doing TV hosting for a new company called StarShop based in New York City when it happened and couldn't get off, so I kept calling Doug for updates. He didn't answer his phone, email or texts for hours. I finally got ahold of Lyndsay, his sister, who told me Doug was chatting away with his ex. Okay, I'll admit it, I did feel a little threatened. And to make matters worse, then I found out she broke up with him while he was away at school. She wanted him to have the "total college experience." Aww, what a selfless sweetheart! That's sarcasm!

3. His last girlfriend before me. Similar to my background, she had no dad and her mom was in jail. But she broke up with

Doug just months before we wed because she'd been married to an alcoholic before and was worried about Doug's former pill problem. Which might explain why Doug was hesitant to tell me, perhaps he thought I'd reject him, too? I did make the mistake of asking him how the sex was with this ex and when he said, "Really good, we really fit together well," I had a moment of internal rage. But I got over it. Her loss, my gain!

By the way, it seems like Doug might have a type. Needy, altruistic nurses or damsels in distress with daddy issues! Okay, I'll admit there was a tiny twinge of jealousy in me about Doug's exes but at least these relationships had taught him valuable lessons that helped our situation. He'd experienced being dumped. I think that's crucial, everyone needs to go through that at least once to have empathy. Doug also didn't seem to initiate breakups—that attitude probably saved our marriage a few times. Plus, I was genuinely relieved that he had been capable of being in monogamous relationships. I didn't want to be married to a player.

Speaking of, Doug and I had the "What's your number?" convo the night we first had sex (only Doug and I talk about other people we slept with before we do it for the first time). We were playing Monopoly and flirting and tipsy, which was kind of the perfect time to talk about how many sexual partners we'd had. Here's a tip: Nobody should be serious and sober—or seriously smashed—when talking about the total number of sex partners. A nice middle ground, a little buzzed and happy, is the key. Otherwise it can get a little accusatory and ugly.

I told Doug that when I was a churchgoing kid, I'd struggled with the thought of waiting until marriage and only having one lover. So I allowed myself the number five. As it turned out, Doug was number five. Awww.

"How many girls have you slept with?" I asked him.

"I don't know!" he said laughing, avoiding, sweating.

"C'mon, you don't know?"

"Fine, maybe 20? 30?"

"Douglas, you can't say both. There's a big difference between 20 and 30!"

He split the difference. I was just ribbing him. I honestly didn't care what the number was, as long as it wasn't, like, over 100 and he didn't have any diseases that would make his penis fall off. Why would I be upset or angry? You can't change the past. It is what it is. And Doug had chosen to be committed to me and I believed that he wanted to only be with me now. I've never understood jealousy. Attractive women are everywhere, a dime a dozen. Your man is going to come into contact with them all day—at work, the store, the gym, everywhere. Why make yourself crazy about it?

At the end of the day, Doug was coming home to me. But when we started having problems, Doug didn't want to come home at all.

The Stan issue started a couple weeks after we got married. At first Doug was supportive. Not long after the experiment ended, we went to Doug's grandpa's funeral. His Grandma Dot, who was my biggest champion, came up to me and grabbed my shoulders.

"You are so good for Doug," she said, staring into my eyes. "He's so happy."

This is no doubt lovely to hear but it scared the crap out of me. I had a panic attack that the family thought we were in love and I knew I wasn't even slightly over Stan. I'm not one to suppress my emotions or lie about how I am truly feeling, so I cried to Doug on the car ride home from his parents' house. I told him that I was doubting myself and our connection. I told him about Stan and my second thoughts.

"Is this real?" I begged to know. "What have we done? Will we last for the long haul?"

He didn't feel threatened or attacked.

"Give love time to grow," he reassured me. "This doesn't happen overnight."

Doug had the patience of a saint, considering I brought up the exact same conversation, oh, another 45 times or so over the next year. I'm not exaggerating. And every time, he'd tell me to have faith and stay the course. The best relationships were a marathon, not a sprint.

I wanted to have the best kind of relationship but I was concerned that we had a fake "TV relationship." One of my biggest issues was that I wasn't convinced that Doug actually loved me. I just couldn't *feel* it at times. Like deep in his bones, heart-vibrating, cray cray love. I refused to live a life of faking a happy marriage and relationship just because our lives are displayed on reality TV. No matter how crazy and loony I seemed I wasn't pretending anything for a TV show. I wanted true, deep, everlasting love. You don't need to download an app to figure out when someone is madly in love with you. It's obvious in their eyes and body language. Maybe I was projecting those thoughts because I was unsure myself. I don't think Doug sincerely felt that I was 100 percent attracted to him and that was a major red flag for him. Not helping matters is that we didn't mention the words "I love you" until the night before we had to film our six-month anniversary special. I told Doug that people would be wondering if we had fallen in love since the experiment ended and if we'd had sex yet. We laughed a little thinking about our stellar experience the night we consummated our marriage, but in true "Damie" style we both clammed up when it came to talking something as serious as love. My heart started pounding and I wanted to tell him "I love you," but I got too shy and clammed up. Before we went to bed, I wish Doug would have rolled over and said sweetly, "Jamie, I love you," but it didn't happen. So the first time we actually said it was on camera during the six-month anniversary special.

After that, we'd say "I love you" all the time but it wasn't intimate or mushy. I also think it's weird that we don't call each other "babe" or "baby," or any of those passionate pet names. I'll call him "my hubby wubby" or "my Dougie Boo Boo." Those are sweet but also kind of jokey. Babe is a term of endearment that has more depth and intimacy. I feel too shy and awkward to say it to Doug and he's never said it to me.

I'd only felt that kind of connection with Stan before. And that was the problem. As time went on, I couldn't stop comparing Doug to Stan.

Stan was always the first person I called when I needed to talk about something. Doug rarely picked up his phone.

Stan would help me talk about deep personal issues. Doug didn't like to go there because it made him uncomfortable.

Stan got out of bed on time in the morning. Doug overslept and had to be dragged out of bed.

Stan knew how to do his taxes. Doug didn't.

Stan felt like a mature partner to me. Doug felt like a child to me.

The more I doubted I could be with Doug forever, the more I gravitated toward Stan. The more I gravitated toward Stan, the more Doug pulled away. Who could blame him? He couldn't win in a matchup with Stan, he felt he wasn't good enough and he got entirely fed up reassuring me every five seconds about everything— that I could trust him, that he didn't just want to get in my pants, that our love was authentic, that I didn't build that connection with Stan overnight, and on and on. He was sick and tired of building me up, only to have me erase it and make him start from scratch all over again.

My biggest flaw was that I was overanalyzing everything to death and in the process, sabotaging our marriage instead of enjoying it. I never let anything just be happy and good because I didn't know the definition of stability. "Of course this won't work out. I married a complete stranger!" was on a loop in my head. The reality was, it could work out if I wasn't so negative. I was the only one causing problems.

Plus, Doug got really ticked off when I criticized his maturity level and whether or not he was responsible enough to be in a long-term relationship. He thought it was vicious and unfair. Doug was hardworking and successful, and he was the one who'd grown up learning about lasting relationships from real role models, two loving parents who'd been together for more than 30 years. Not to mention, his grandparents had been married over 40 years.

So, he absolutely despised when I'd question his manhood. It caused heated arguments. No, he wasn't Stan, he'd argue, but why should he be? Comparing them was like apples and oranges. "You have selfish expectations of me," he complained. "You are the most selfish person I've ever seen. How are you so perfect? What more do I have to do? I give and give and give and you never ask what I want or give back to me. Your image of the perfect man is unrealistic."

Stan was not perfect by any means, he'd never even been able to commit to me wholeheartedly. And yet, in my head, I'd put him up on a pedestal. He could do no wrong. Everything Doug did was wrong, even though he had committed to me for the rest of my life. Yet, he wasn't good enough.

In Doug's mind, we were in quicksand, at a toxic breaking point. "What the fuck am I doing?" he thought. He wasn't happy. He didn't see a light at the end of the tunnel. A major shift happened. He stopped giving a shit. He started being passive aggressive. His lateness got wildly out of control and he had no intention of changing. Was this my forever? Like, once we have kids it'll be even worse and we'll be five hours late to everything? It got to the point that when Doug was dawdling, I'd go sit in the car and wait for him. But the more I encouraged him to hurry up, the longer he'd take.

The worst it ever got was when my sister asked him to officiate her wedding. It was a quick wedding being that she only gave us a month's notice. Doug said he was honored and of course he would. I was thrilled that my sister wanted my husband to have such an important role in her wedding. When the weekend arrived, I went upstate without Doug to help set up and prepare. Doug said he had to work but promised he'd make the four-hour trip the morning of the wedding. Two hours before my sister and her future husband were supposed to say, "I do," Doug still had not arrived. Frantic, I bombarded him with calls and messages asking where the ef he was. Low and behold, Doug missed the rehearsal they had planned. I mean, how could he be so careless to miss the whole rehearsal when he is the minister officiating the ceremony AND he didn't show up to officiate my sister's wedding until 10 minutes before she had to walk down the aisle? To make matters worse he left before the reception even began. He said he had a softball game to get to. It was a memorial game that he just couldn't miss. So while everyone was dancing with their partners I was sitting by myself thinking. Bad idea. I was embarrassed, hurt, and enraged. I get that my sister's wedding was last minute and unexpected, but so was ours. And when we were getting married we only gave two weeks notice for our families. My sister dropped everything to be there for us. We should have done the same for her. Clearly he gave two shits about my family or me.

And here's the "more" I promised you about Stan. This all happened after I invited Doug to Stan's album release concert. Surprise, he didn't want to go. Doug and I had pushed our marriage to the brink. Miserable and vulnerable, I showed up at Stan's gig by myself with my sisters, only to come face-to-face with his girlfriend. It was the first time I was at one of Stan's concerts and I wasn't his girlfriend.

"That used to be me," I secretly thought, my heart sinking like a stone.

All sorts of feelings came flooding back and I felt the stab of yearning. I realized I missed being Stan's band babe and now this woman had stepped into my shoes. The show stirred up intense emotions in me. My husband should have been by my side yet was nowhere to be found. I tried to push my feelings for Stan way down deep but it was impossible. I wanted to be the one by his side cheering for him and caring for him. Stan had always supported me in everything I had ever done and had always been by my side. I wished I had never left his.

When I got back to New Jersey, I walked in the door, Doug was engrossed in some show, eating on a TV tray, and barely noticed I was back.

"Helloooooooo?"

I slunk off to bed alone and lay there thinking about my ex. I knew it was so wrong. I felt like I was cheating mentally. Even if I wasn't physically having an affair, this was not okay either way. I loved Doug, but I wasn't in love with him the way I was in love with Stan.

Doug and I needed to have the most serious talk we'd ever had.

I was pretty certain we were over.

Just over a year into our marriage, we sat down in our living room on the couch to talk about getting a divorce. We did not scream and throw things. It was worse. We were quiet and calm. I was used to screaming and throwing things, so quiet condescending jabs were even more dramatic and hurtful.

"I don't think you care to understand me."

"We don't have a real connection. We're just *there.*"

"We're not nice to each other."

"Why are we even together? What is the deal?"

Doug paused, then he unleashed the wolves.

"What would it look like if went our separate ways?"

We talked about all of the logistics, like where we'd live, and I offered to give my engagement ring back. "No, you can keep it," he said. Custody of Lady was the toughest topic, because she was my dog but had come to worship Doug.

"We'll always be friends," I said.

"If we divorce," Doug said, "we will not be friends."

"What do you mean? I'm friends with Stan."

Ugh, why did I bring him up?

"No," Doug said.

It was the (figurative) punch in the stomach I needed. Oh my God, no this can't be—I'd miss him too much. It was the first sign that I loved him more than I thought I did. When we fought we fought hard, but when we loved our love was *so* much stronger. I went to bed heartbroken and so angry at myself and this whole situation.

The next morning Doug emailed me from work and, TMI, I got it on the way to pee and read it on the toilet. He was always so much better writing his feelings and I do my best thinking sitting on the can:

Jamie,

I want to apologize for yesterday, and I am sorry that you felt the way you did, but you really never gave me a chance to explain. What really upsets me is how I still have not earned your trust. After all that we have been through, and all that we have done together, I made a commitment to you, and I want this to work.

This makes me feel like one of those guys, and it is really upsetting that you put me in that category, the same category as an asshole guy from your past, and someone that is trying to manipulate or hurt you. I have NONE of those characteristics. I am not that kind of person. I am not out to hurt you, or manipulate you! I am your husband, and someone that loves you!

Marriage is a team effort, and each person shares equal responsibility, equal blame, and you build a life together. There is no question that we are going through a rough patch, and it seems to get harder and harder to get back on track. It is going to take both of us to get this back on track!

Lately it seems as though the times that I annoy you have far out-weighed the times that you are happy with me, and I don't know what to do, I feel like there is no winning with you. I cannot remember the last time that we went through a whole day completely and totally happy. I take a lot of the blame, and I am at fault too! I know there are times that I am annoying, and times that I am less sensitive to the situation.

I have been very patient and open to compromise, but I feel like that is all that I am doing, and I am seeing absolutely nothing in return.

I started to think about how much that I have compromised, and how much that I have given and whether or not any of that mattered to you? Then I started to think about me and my needs. That is what compelled me to write down my thoughts.

I have tried so hard to make you happy, and I have tried so hard to show you that I love you, and that I care about you but it seems like all of that effort falls on deaf ears, and no matter what good I do, ALL of that can be wiped away by something that annoys you, or something that bothers you. I try to learn from my mistakes, and grow with you, but in all honesty, I feel like you have not even tried to compromise, or tried to be a little more "easygoing," or tried to get over some of the little things.

I started to think about when the last time you went out of your way to do something special for me, or did something that was thoughtful for me...and the sad part is that I can't. I can't remember the last time you showed me any real love or affection. I am not talking about sex at all. When the last time you rubbed my back, or showed me ANY affection.

JAMIE OTIS | Wifey 101

I don't require much Jamie, and I am saying these things because I want things to change. I want us to be great together. I want to get through this. I am willing to do whatever is needed to get us back on track.

But I have to know that you want the same?

If you put yourself in my shoes for a minute, it hurts for me to write this, but I haven't felt like you were proud of me as your husband in a really long time. I know that some of the romance and intimacy is awkward for you but I can't remember ever feeling wanted by you, like you were attracted to me, like I was special to you.

Here is my heart on my sleeve. I am saying that I am willing to work with you, AS A TEAM, to get us to a good place, and I will give this everything I got if you are willing to give the same!

Otherwise, I cannot continue like this!

I genuinely hope from the bottom of my heart that this is one of those things that we work together to get past, and it makes us stronger in the end.

I love you Jamie, and always will no matter what! I will put 1,000% of my blood, sweat and tears into making this work!

I just hope you feel the same!

I started bawling. Like the worst ugly crying you've ever seen. He was right. What have I done for him? When was the last time I went out of my way to show him I loved him and cared about him? All of my focus has been on ME, ME, ME. What is right for ME? Who is right for ME? At the end of day I'm married to an incredible man. Why am I obsessing over Stan?

Soon after this Doug decided to have a guys' night so I went to one of my best friend Noha's apartment. When I walked in I must've looked a bit down and out because Noha immediately asked, "What's wrong?" Gee, I didn't know it was *that* obvious. I told her everything was fine but she gave me that look like "Yeah, ok. And now the real answer." I'd been friends with Noha for years. We did a pageant together and hit it off immediately. "Jamie, your wedding vow renewal just aired on national television. You should be over the moon right now. What's going on?" She was right. I told her I just didn't know how serious Doug was and that I remember my relationship with Stan being so much more serious even if we weren't married. And to that Noha gave me the figurative slap across the face that I needed. She said, "You have an amazing husband. He has always been there for you. Yet, you never let him in fully. You never even gave him a full chance. It's almost like you've been testing him and your relationship since the day you said 'I do.'" She was right. My habit of having "one foot out the door" had followed me into my marriage. And because we were complete strangers being legally married at first sight by four experts I just assumed it wouldn't work anyway. As much as I wanted a happy marriage and a big welcoming family I didn't believe that the way I got it was *real* and would *last*. I mean, c'mon, I got married on TV. It all seemed way too good to be true. I didn't want to get my heart broken so instead of opening it I guarded it. But that's not fair to Doug because he put himself out there and accepted me and my family with his whole heart immediately.

This was a HUGE wake-up call. I began looking back at all the times Doug put his hand out and I just pushed it away. There were so many times Doug was patient as a saint as I tried to work out issues with my mom and my past. Why had I been so difficult in our marriage? Why didn't I thank him and love him for all he's done instead of seemingly punishing him? Gosh, I felt like the most screwed up individual. I couldn't let my marriage end and fizzle knowing I had never even given it a chance. I knew Doug was an amazing man. Why had I been so guarded and assumed it'd all fail before we even really got started? What was wrong with me?!

Thank God Noha and I had the kind of friendship where she could speak the God's honest truth to me without worrying she'd hurt my feelings. She didn't care as long as she got through to me. She did.

Noha flat out told me, "You suck. You're not going to make it if you don't change."

She was right. I knew this but refused to accept it. Stan was not the right guy for me. If he was, we would have already been together. Doug and I were really right for each other in so many ways. The only thing holding us back from a wonderful future was me and all of my issues and hand wringing and hemming and hawing.

Doug had voluntarily married me and had stuck it out for more than a year, despite the fact that I'd been the worst kind of high-maintenance witchy poo. Nobody had ever come close to sticking with me like that before. He was patient and loving and generous and funny and smart. He didn't care that I woke up with mascara smeared on my eyes. Or that I had mood swings. He'd proven over and over again that he cared about me. He wanted to be my husband.

In return, I expected perfection and wanted to bolt any time he showed a minor flaw. Every couple has problems; it's just a matter of time before they reveal themselves. In our little TV experiment bubble, our issues rose to the surface quickly and simultaneously. They were overwhelming because of the time frame but they weren't serious issues that couldn't be worked on and resolved.

For some reason, I'd convinced myself that my husband should have 100 percent of the qualities I'd put on a MASH game when I was like twelve. But that's preposterous. Nobody can live up to those expectations. Life is not all rainbows and butterflies. People disappoint, that's in our natures. If you find a partner who has 60 percent of the qualities you want—and they don't beat you, get arrested, cheat or have addiction issues—you're lucky. That's not settling. That's being happy.

After talking with Doug and Noha, I knew what I wanted. I wanted Doug to be my husband forever. But I didn't know if it was too late. When he didn't bring the divorce up again, sweeping it under the rug in true Dougie fashion, thank God, I had time to consciously make an effort to change my behavior. I hadn't been a good wife. That's an understatement. I wanted to be the best wife and give 150 percent. I had wanted immediate rainbows and butterflies after changing my last name, but clearly I didn't put in enough work. Now I knew that it would take making a conscious effort *daily*. I couldn't change what Doug was doing but I could change what I was doing. And at this point I needed to be patient with Doug until I proved to him that I believed in our marriage and us. So this is what I did:

1. I stopped talking about Stan with Doug. Any comparison to him was unfair. (Hallelujah!)

2. I stopped pointing out Doug's flaws.

3. I let Doug sleep in as late as he wanted, with no agenda.

4. I didn't let my thoughts run wild about whether or not we were right for each other. I trusted that we were and stopped feeding into negative thoughts.

5. I tried to have more fun in our sex life. I greeted Doug naked at the front door one night after work and I even donned cute lingerie.

6. I stopped complaining and being grouchy. He came home to a happy woman and that made him happy.

7. I brushed my hair and looked presentable. I know this sounds crazy but maybe he didn't want to see me in my

sweatpants 24/7. I know this because he actually said to me, "Every time I see you, you're in sweatpants." And then he gave me a kiss.

8. I cooked, cleaned, and made sure he had coffee every morning before work. That doesn't make me an anti-feminist. It made me a good, caring partner.

9. I stopped talking to my ex. It was time to let go. Doug would never have asked me to, he's never been controlling about that, but it was the right thing to do.

10. I made Doug my best friend. All the things I thought I couldn't talk to Doug about, turns out I could.

At first, I couldn't feel or see a difference and I got impatient. Why is this not better already? Why are we not on Cloud 9? Well, think about a building demolition. It takes seconds to blow it up and months to build something back up on the foundation again.

I expected a miracle to happen overnight but it took incremental changes over months to finally see results. For the first time, I didn't say, "Screw it." I hung in there and one day, out of the blue, Doug made changes, too. He didn't have to, most of this was really my fault. But he started being on time because he wanted to. He even acknowledged to me that he respects me enough to know it hurts me and embarrasses me when we are late to events. He also started making an effort to save money. One day he came home with a used Wii and bragged about how it was just as good as a new one and he saved $300. Our favorite games to play are still good ol' *Mario Brothers*, by the way.

We took baby steps to save our marriage and it happened naturally. Before, Doug practically needed an instruction manual to do our marriage right in my eyes. How could we fall in love organically when every moment we had was so contrived? We gravitated back to the middle. I chilled out a little and Doug stepped up. It was a long process to change our bad behavior to good behavior. It was not a quick easy fix and we knew it would be constant work going forward. We made consistent changes daily. I lowered my unreasonable expectations, began therapy for the struggles I've gone through and my own insecurities about not *feeling* truly loved, and suddenly, one day, we were back to being Team Damie. Slowly but surely our relationship got better and our love grew stronger.

I knew it because *I felt it* in my bones.

CHAPTER 10

Introducing Henley
Hehner?

As I type, Doug and I have just celebrated our second wedding
anniversary on March 23. Which I believe is "cotton," unless you
choose to go by the modern symbol "china," and if you do, I don't
blame you. A quick search of Etsy.com for cotton anniversary gifts
shows a lot of towels, bathrobes and pillows, which Doug just bought
last week at Bed Bath & Beyond without a 20 percent off coupon, so
thanks but no thanks. He's still working on the money thing and I've
learned to just let.it.go. It's not that big of a deal at the end of the day.

Making it two years—that's 104 weeks or 730 days—is not about the material stuff anyway. Who would have thunk that we would have made it this far? It's a miracle. Not a Mother Teresa kind of miracle but relatively speaking, it's pretty darn astonishing, considering our dubious start in a scientifically arranged marriage. Looking back, what a whirlwind of craziness!

Doug and I worked our butts off to keep this love train on the track. Is hard work the reason we made it, while many of the other couples crashed and burned and went their separate ways? Of course not; it's not that simple. Was it chemistry? Stubbornness? Fear of failure? Impossible to say. It's futile to try to understand the connection between two people. What I do know is that Doug and I went into this with sincere intentions. We genuinely wanted to be married. And once we were, we genuinely wanted to fall in love.

We fell in and out of love several times. There's no question that we would have broken up if we were just dating. That darn piece of paper kept us together and made us hang in there just a little longer and try just a little harder. We learned that falling in love again with the *same* person is a bazillion times better than searching through strangers and having to go on tons of dates to find love. And this is kind of a no-brainer, but it also makes your marriage a million times stronger and more secure.

Here's what else we learned:

- *Your marriage will have peaks and valleys.*

- *Do not expect problems to be solved overnight.*

- *It's not in our DNA to be happy 100 percent of the time so deal with it.*

It's true that some marriages are just not meant to last and that's fine. How do you know whether or not to pull the plug? I knew Doug was the one for me, despite all of the issues we were dealing with, because he kissed me every morning, even when I had morning breath, and birds' nest hair and mascara smeared all over my eyes when I was too lazy to take my makeup off. We weathered the worst storms and came out the other side respecting each other rather than hating the sight of each other. Even when I was the worst person to live with, he still was willing to try to understand me and work together with me. Even though I wasn't always excited to see him after work, and I didn't always want to have sex with him, he was so patient and respectful of me. I loved his family. Which is not a good enough reason in and of itself but it's a major bonus, the cherry on top. He always wanted to see me do better and was willing to help, expecting nothing in return. We balanced each other—he was laid back and I was high strung. He always had my back, and loved me when I wasn't my best self, but he also held me accountable if I acted like a weenie. He gave me space. He appreciated my strength and ambition and independence. He doesn't care that I legally changed my name to Hehner but don't use it publicly because I decided to embrace my identity. He actually told me to keep my name Jamie Otis public since no one knows me as Jamie Hehner. I really like having the ability to be Jamie Hehner in my private life. Besides, I changed my last name for us, not for the public. One day when we have kids we will all have the same last name and that is all that matters.

Most important, I could not imagine celebrating holidays and birthdays without him.

Maybe if you're in your early 20s you can go back out there and try to trade up. But I'm not gonna lie, it gets harder as you get older to find a quality partner. I used to jump out of relationships instead of trying to work it out. That got me nowhere. Ultimately, I hung on to Doug for dear life because he's a great man who shares the same values as I do.

Wow, Doug's head should be swelling like a Macy's Thanksgiving Day Parade balloon right about now. Again he's not perfect. His chronic lateness and bad credit were difficult to deal with. But he was willing to try harder to be better. And that is the key in our relationship. Just the other day, for the first time ever, he let me open his bills and help him sort them out. He thought his student loan was being automatically deducted from his account but it wasn't and he was months behind. We paid the balance and now he's caught up.

Because we've both worked so hard at self-improvement in the areas that were driving each other crazy, we reached a major milestone. Just last summer, during the peak of our problems, I'd spent a ridiculous amount of time and energy house hunting. As typical with Doug, he didn't say much while I was obliviously and blissfully searching for our dream home. When I found a house I fell in love with, which had lots of land for horses, I was ready to put in an offer. Only then did Doug finally voice his opinion. "I don't want to buy a house with you," he stated firmly. When he put the hammer down, I was furious. I had wasted so much time and embarrassed myself to the Realtor, our family friend, who now probably thought I'd wasted her time, too. But gosh darn it if Doug wasn't right. We were nowhere near ready to make that kind of life-changing purchase together for a variety of valid reasons, including his bad credit and our relationship being as stable as an earthquake. Doug was usually so go-with-the-flow about everything. This time, when it really mattered, he wasn't. He was so smart about it, it made me respect him so much.

Finally, after nearly two years filled with the highest highs and the lowest lows, Doug and I are the most solid and secure in our relationship we've ever been. Having two people who love and forgave whole heartedly was key, but I'm not going to lie, going to therapy has also been very helpful. I'm happy to report that Doug and I recently agreed it was time to start looking for a new house.

I'm also happy to report that Doug asked me if we could start trying to have a baby on our vacation in South Africa, his final activity on his pre-baby bucket list!

Not long ago, we'd been in the same predicament about bringing a little Hehner into the world. Fans, our in-laws, everyone kept asking when we were going to get pregnant. Like many (dumb) desperate people in troubled marriages, I thought having a baby might save our relationship and make so many people happy. Until my sister Leah knocked some sense into me. "A baby does not fix it!" she yelled at me. "It makes it ten times worse!" So we waited.

I'm so glad we waited. Leah's right. It's really not wise to bring a baby into the world unless both parents are 100 percent ready and excited about it. (Do I even have to say that? Yes, people like me think it may "fix" your issues.) Doug has always been hesitant. I decided that until he was the one asking me for a baby I wanted to wait. And, he was right. Why on earth did I even want to bring a kiddo into our rocky relationship?

After nearly a year of working on our relationship we are finally back in love more than ever before. I know this because I can *feel* it in my bones, in my soul. It's not what he does or says, but just how he *is*. It's the way he looks at me. The way he spoons me. The way he has always loved me unconditionally. How he has never judged me for being less than a perfect wife and a bit whack-a-doodle at times. Recently Doug and I had a heart to heart…text. Doug's always been better talking about his feelings in writing.

Me: I'm making a doc apt for a physical. I could have my IUD taken out (birth control)…Should I? Be honest and tell me how you truly feel lol.

Doug: Sam is doing a bday party for Bill on the 23rd, somewhere in New Brunswick, we don't have anything right?

Me: We can def go

Me: Way to change the subject lol

Doug: You should have it taken out, and we just have to be responsible using condoms. But it's been in there too long, and I support that decision!

Me: Really?!?! You know that makes us one step closer, right? And condoms aren't as reliable as an IUD.

Doug: Yes, I do!

I wanted to make sure Doug was serious and certain. When he got home that night from work I asked him again. "Are you sure you're ok with this? This means now we have to use condoms every time or we may get pregnant." Doug said, "I know." But we've never used condoms. Not once as long as we've been married. I looked at him and said, "You know we aren't going to use condoms." He looked back at me and smiled, "I know." So there you go. We are officially ready and trying to have a baby! Go ahead and cry—or laugh at this text and conversation because we have many times. I'm so incredibly thrilled but I'm also so scared. My biggest fear is that I have bad karma and won't be able to get pregnant because of my abortions. I'm nervous about finances. I'm nervous about raising a child in this dangerous, topsy-turvy world right now. I'm nervous it's not the right time. We still need to buy a home. But as Doug's dad told me, he lost his job when Bonnie got pregnant. It's going to be okay.

It's like that old saying, if everybody waited for the right time to have a baby, you'd never have one. I have to remember where I came from, too. If my mom could have babies, I could *definitely* have babies.

The one thing I'm not nervous about at all is being a mother. I think I'm going to be a great mom. I have a lot of people who are willing to share their advice—my mother-in-law, my sisters, and my friends. Plus, I've already done it once with my siblings and I made so many mistakes that I learned from and I know I'll never repeat them again. I'm the first to admit I really sucked at being a parental figure the first time around (Sorry Amy, Leah, and Dale!)—I had no idea what I was doing—but I'm grateful for the experience. And I think deep down my siblings are grateful I stepped up, even if I seemed like a tyrant sometimes. It was my way or the highway.

Here are some "never again" promises I'm making for little Henley Hehner (that's a joke, we will not name our firstborn after the wrong name I called Doug on our wedding night! Or maybe we will…Douglas?). True story: We woke up after being married for one day and Doug said to me "You're Jamie Nicole Otis." I looked at him and said "And you're Douglas Edward…Henley?" Oh goodness. One day in and I was already getting it wrong—or did I get it right? At least the right name for our first baby? Our firstborn can print this out and tape it to our refrigerator to hold me accountable:

I PROMISE to always, always, always be there for you.

I PROMISE to love you unconditionally, forever.

I PROMISE to not make impossible-to-complete to-do lists.

I PROMISE to say thank you for completing chores.

I PROMISE to not expect you to be perfect.

I PROMISE to not harp on mistakes for weeks.

I PROMISE to not spoil you to make up for my childhood neglect.

I PROMISE to let you follow your own path.

One of the biggest mistakes I made was expecting my siblings to have the same dreams as me and that wasn't fair. I wanted them all to graduate from high school, but news flash, when you move from school to school and have no set friends and are bullied by the kids there is nothing wrong with "dropping out" and getting your GED. I tried to force them to go to college and college is just not for everyone. The route from A to B has many paths but I had tunnel vision. My sister wanted to be a military nurse and I begged her not to join the Navy because we were at war. I loved her and wanted her to succeed, but I was scared that she may be hurt while training or worse, killed while deployed. Even though those are legit worries, that doesn't make it ok that I deterred her from her goal of being a nurse in the Navy. It was very selfish of me. She wandered around aimlessly for awhile after that because I pooh-pooh'd her dream. I told her she could become a nurse the same way I did—through college. What I've learned since then is that it's okay to not follow a traditional route.

It was really hypocritical of me, considering I have not taken a traditional route in life at all and I've succeeded beyond my wildest dreams. (After writing this book I've had my eyes opened to this hypocritical side of me. Geesh, I'm going to work on this pronto because it's not very becoming!)

I'm a registered nurse and a TV host. I've become a successful entrepreneur and created a beautiful jewelry line. Best of all, I've got an awesome marriage that I finally believe in regardless of what others think or the unconventional way we met. We *LOVE* each other and that is the only thing that matters. After working hard and fighting to figure out "how to be married" for our first two years of marriage I've learned to hold myself more accountable, but also to give myself some credit for doing the best I know how. Sure you definitely need trust, faith, loyalty, commitment, but another thing I've learned is that you've gotta relax and have FUN in marriage. One thing's for certain, every day I wake up trying my best to be a great wife. And I cannot wait to be a loving mom to my own little ones. Fingers crossed we get our first baby Hehner soon!

ACKNOWLEDGMENTS

I would like to thank my hubby wubby, Douglas Hehner, for endless love and support. Linda King, Johanna Harvey, AmyLynn Lucas, Leah King, Dale King, Bonnie Hehner, Doug Hehner, Lyndsay Hehner, Joe Zizza, Matt Hehner, Kerri Hehner, Elya Whitmore, Noha Moussa, Heather Elwell, Kirstyn Peterson, Kate Wogas, Sara Saubier, Elena Schelich, Lonnie Park, and all of my friends who hold me accountable, love me and support me—thank you. Huge thanks to everyone at FYI Network with a special shout-out to Liz Fine, Heddy Gold, James Bolosh, Gena McCarthy, Heather Pastorini, Caitlin Van Mol, and Jana Bennett. Another BIG thank you to everyone at Kinetic productions—Chris Coelen, Sam Dean, Brenda Coston, Anneli Gallick, Annie Pandaru, Carly Scher, Katie Zakula, Paria Sagdighi and the whole crew. I'd like to thank my agent, Mark

Turner. Last but definitely not least: I am overwhelmingly thankful to my cowriter Dibs Baer. We make one heck of a team!

Dibs would like to thank Linda Baer, Brett and Cathy Baer, Sam Horn, Khali MacIntyre and Potsch Boyd, Courtney Robertson, Ever Mainard, Bro Haus, Melissa Cronin, Marianne Garvey, Marisa Sullivan, Casey Brennan, Scooter and Fiona, Michelle Meyers and Robin Strober, and the gang at Next Level Fitness.

ABOUT THE AUTHORS

Jamie Otis is a registered nurse working in labor and delivery at Columbia Presbyterian Medical Center. She's the host of Married At First Sight: Unfiltered and the creator of Jamie Otis Jewelry. She's appeared on Dr. Drew, Dr. Oz, The View, Good Morning America, and The Today Show with Kathie Lee Gifford and Hoda Kotb. She met her husband, Doug Hehner, on the popular TV show Married At First Sight. She lives in New Jersey with her hubby and their two rescue pups, Foxy and Lady.

DIBS BAER is the co-author of the *New York Times* bestselling book *I Didn't Come Here to Make Friends: Confessions of a Reality Show Villain*. Dibs is the former executive editor of *In Touch Weekly* and has recently profiled celebrities for the covers of *Women's Health* and *Vegas* magazines. She lives in LA & Palm Springs with her dog Scooter.

41862434R00132

Made in the USA
San Bernardino, CA
22 November 2016